MW01068497

Indiana Bucket List Adventure Guide

Explore 100 Offbeat Destinations You Must Visit!

Kristen Bennett

Canyon Press
canyon@purplelink.org

Please consider writing a review!
Just visit: purplelink.org/review

Copyright 2022. Canyon Press. All Rights Reserved.
No part of this book may be reproduced or transmitted in any form or
by any means, electronic or mechanical, including photocopying,
recording or by any other form without written permission from the
publisher.

ISBN: 978-1-957590-14-1

FREE BONUS

Discover 31 Incredible Places You Can
Visit Next! Just Go To:

purplelink.org/travel

Table of Contents:

Gary

Hammond

How to Use This Book

Welcome to your very own adventure guide to exploring the many wonders of the state of Indiana. Not only does this book present the most wonderful places to visit and sights to see in the vast state, but it provides GPS coordinates for Google Maps to make exploring that much easier.

Adventure Guide
Sorted by region, this guide offers over 100 amazing wonders found in Indiana for you to see and explore. They can be visited in any order and this book will help you keep track of where you've been and where to look forward to going next. Each section describes the area or place and what to look for and also tells you the physical address, and what you may need to bring along.

GPS Coordinates
As you can imagine, not all of the locations in this book have a physical address. Fortunately, some of our listed wonders are either located within a National Park or Reserve, or near a city, town, or place of business. For those that are not associated with a specific location, it is easiest to map it using GPS coordinates.

Luckily, Google has a system of codes that converts the coordinates into pin-drop locations that Google Maps can interpret and navigate.

Each adventure in this guide includes GPS coordinates along with a physical address whenever it is available.

It is important that you are prepared for poor cell signals, so it is recommended that you route your location and ensure that the directions are accessible offline. Depending on your device and the distance of some locations, you may need to travel with a backup battery source.

About Indiana

Known as the Hoosier State, Indiana entered the Union in 1816 as the 19th state. It was originally home to the Illini, Shawnee, and Miami Native American tribes, and several still call the state home today. French explorer Samuel de Chaplain became one of the first Europeans to set foot in Indiana in 1614, and by the late 17th century, the French controlled the entire area.

During the French and Indian War (1754–1763), the English fought the French for control of the region and ended up winning what would later become known as the Indiana Territory. Following the conclusion of the American Revolution in 1783, England ceded Indiana to the Americans, paving the way for it to become part of the Union.

While Indiana was named for the Native American tribes who were living in the territory when Europeans arrived, the origins of the nickname "Hoosier" are less clear. The word was first used to describe a person who lived in the hills of Indiana in the 1820s and may have derived from an old English slang word that means "hill."

One of the most popular events in the state is the Indianapolis 500, a 500-mile car race that has been held annually in the state's capital since 1911 (except for 6 years during World War I and World War II). It encompasses 200 laps of 2.5 miles each and is held at the Indianapolis Motor Speedway.

Famous people who hail from Indiana include NBA player Larry Bird, actor James Dean, political activist Eugene V.

Debs, authors Theodore Dreiser and Kurt Vonnegut, and presidents Benjamin Harrison, William Henry Harrison, and Abraham Lincoln, among others.

Landscape and Climate

Located in the Midwestern U.S., Indiana is bordered by four states: Michigan to the north, Kentucky to the south and east, Ohio to the east, and Illinois to the west. Lake Michigan is also a northern neighbor. The state itself is divided into three main regions.

The northern portion of the state is the Great Lakes Plains region, which is characterized by sand dunes, lakes, and low hills. The Till Plains region in the center of the state is often considered part of the "Corn Belt" because of its corn crops. This area features low hills, valleys, and Hoosier Hill, the state's highest point.

In the southern part of the state, the Southern Plains and Lowlands regions are characterized by steep hills juxtaposed against lowlands, limestone caverns, and the Ohio River, which marks the state's southern border. Indiana is packed with natural resources such as coal, gas, and oil, and there are numerous gravel, sand, and limestone quarries.

Categorized as a hot-summer, humid continental climate, summers in Indiana can range from mild to hot. High temperatures in the daytime hover around the low to mid-80s, but the frequent humidity can make it feel significantly hotter. Precipitation is fairly consistent throughout the year, but the southern cities usually see a few more inches of rain than those in the north.

Severe weather can be an issue in the spring and fall, particularly during peak tornado season in the spring. Flooding can also be a problem from March through May, and the fall is often the driest, sunniest, and least humid time of the year. Lake-effect snow occurs frequently in the winter up near Lake Michigan and can extend as far south as the middle of the state.

January is the coldest month of the year, with average daytime temperatures in the mid-30s. The lows overnight average in the upper teens.

Mounds State Park

This fascinating state park is home to 10 amazing earthworks that were constructed by prehistoric Native Americans known as the Adena-Hopewell tribe. The largest of the earthworks, the Great Mound, is estimated to have been built circa 160 BCE. According to archaeologists, the mounds were likely used as gathering places for spiritual ceremonies, as astronomical alignments can be viewed from these structures. A nature center is also located in Mounds State Park. It offers animal exhibits, interactive games, a wildlife-viewing area, and much more. Hiking is also available throughout the park, and naturalist-led treks and interpretive programs are offered on the weekends.

Best Time to Visit: The best time to visit Mounds State Park is on the weekends in the spring or fall to take advantage of the programs offered by the nature center during mild weather.

Pass/Permit/Fees: There is a $7 fee for in-state vehicles and a $9 fee for out-of-state vehicles. There is also a $2 fee per person for walk-ins.

Closest City or Town: Anderson

Physical Address: 4306 Mounds Road, Anderson, IN 46017

GPS Coordinates: 40.10102° N, 85.61974° W

Did You Know? An amusement park that exploited the mounds occupied what is now Mounds State Park from 1897 to 1929.

Pokagon State Park

Originally named Lake James State Park when it was proposed in 1925, Indiana's fifth state park was eventually called Pokagon State Park to honor the Native American culture that existed in the area before the Europeans arrived. Pokagon is the surname of the last two notable leaders of the Potawatomi Native American tribe to reside here. Two lakes, Lake James and Snow Lake, border the park and offer excellent fishing, boating, and swimming opportunities. The park is also popular in the winter because it boasts some of the best cross-country skiing, ice fishing, and sledding in the state. It also has a twin-track toboggan run for thrill-seekers who want to experience 35–40 miles per hour on an icy track. There are nine hiking trails throughout the park as well, all varying in difficulty.

Best Time to Visit: Summer is great for water activities and hiking, but winter is best for using the toboggan run.

Pass/Permit/Fees: There is a $7 fee for in-state vehicles and a $9 fee for out-of-state vehicles. There is also a $2 fee per person for walk-ins.

Closest City or Town: Angola

Physical Address: 450 Lane 100, Lake James, Angola, IN 46703

GPS Coordinates: 41.70821° N, 85.02282° W

Did You Know? You can find lodging at the park at the 40-room Potawatomi Inn, which dates back to 1927.

Portland Arch

The Portland Arch is a 435-acre natural area adjacent to the Wabash River. One of just a few natural arches in the state, it was created by Bear Creek, which undercut the sandstone bluffs on both sides of its banks. The arch was formed approximately 230 million years ago during the Pennsylvanian Period. It was likely used as shelter by Native Americans and early European pioneers. The state nature preserve was dedicated in 1972 and has remained in a natural state of forests, cliffs, wetlands, prairies, and savannas since then. The trail to the arch is 1.8 miles in length and meanders along Bear Creek. A wide variety of plant species can be seen along the path, including wintergreen, huckleberry, honeysuckle, and the only Indiana-grown Canada blueberries in the state. Before becoming a nature preserve, the area was home to a resort and then a Boy Scout camp, both of which are long gone.

Best Time to Visit: The best time to visit is during the spring or fall when the weather is mild.

Pass/Permit/Fees: There is no fee to visit the arch.

Closest City or Town: Attica

Physical Address: 1599 W. Scout Camp Road, Covington, IN 47932

GPS Coordinates: 40.22046° N, 87.33602° W

Did You Know? The Portland Arch was named for the town of Portland, Indiana, which has since been renamed Fountain.

Wolf Park

This educational and research facility has been operating in Battle Ground, Indiana since 1972. Its purpose is to study the behavior of wolves and other wild dogs. Thousands of visitors come to Wolf Park each year to learn about the importance of wolves and other predators in the ecosystem. One way that the park helps researchers is by providing a comparative environment to the wild to illustrate the behavioral differences between captive and wild animals. The park is home to numerous animals, including wolves, foxes, coyotes, and bison. Their enclosures are considered semi-natural, and the animals have been socialized to feel comfortable around humans. This does not mean they are tamed, so visitors are not allowed to interact with them. However, visitors can get close looks at these animals.

Best Time to Visit: The park is open Sunday through Friday from 9:30 a.m. to 2:30 p.m. and Saturday from 9:30 a.m. to 9:00 p.m.

Pass/Permit/Fees: The Follow the Pack Tour is $10 for adults and $8 for children between the ages of 6 and 13. Other tours and events may have different rates.

Closest City or Town: Battle Ground

Physical Address: 4004 E. 800 North, Battle Ground, IN 47920

GPS Coordinates: 40.53470° N, 86.83036° W

Did You Know? Howl Night allows visitors to enjoy the howls of wolves in their habitats.

Bluespring Caverns

This karst cave system consists of 21 miles of surveyed passages and has the longest subterranean river in the country. It was discovered in the 19th century, but up until 1913, the cave's entrance was located by a spring that drained into the White River. A dam that was completed in 1913 closed off this entrance, and a second entrance was created following a severe storm in 1940. A pond located on George Colglazier's farm vanished into a sinkhole and became the present-day cave entrance. Colglazier's sons explored the cave frequently and then began to welcome visitors to the area to descend underground for free. These days, guests can take a 17-person boat on the subterranean river to tour the caverns, which are the third longest in Indiana.

Best Time to Visit: The caverns are only open between April 1 and October 31 from 9:00 a.m. to 5:00 p.m.

Pass/Permit/Fees: Admission is $20 for adults and $12 for children under the age of 15.

Closest City or Town: Bedford

Physical Address: 1459 Blue Springs Cavern Road, Bedford, IN 47421

GPS Coordinates: 38.79846° N, 86.54681° W

Did You Know? The Colglazier family never profited from the Bluespring Caverns on their property, and they only had one rule, which was "not to destroy or remove from the caverns."

Hoosier National Forest Caves

Located in the 200,000-acre Hoosier National Forest, the caves are open on a seasonal basis for public exploration. For visitors who love the dark mysteries of the underground world, the numerous caves in the forest provide endless recreation. These caves are not commercially operated, so if you do decide to explore a cave during the open season, be sure to take safety precautions. For instance, never go caving alone, dress in multiple layers of clothing, wear sturdy shoes, bring multiple light sources and a first aid kit, and don't forget to carry enough food and water for several days in case you get trapped. More than 54 animal species have been found in the Hoosier National Forest Caves, which provide a unique and fragile ecosystem for these creatures.

Best Time to Visit: The only time you can visit the caves is between May 1 and August 31 each year.

Pass/Permit/Fees: There is no fee to visit the caves.

Closest City or Town: Bedford

Physical Address: 811 Constitution Avenue, Bedford, IN 47421

GPS Coordinates: 38.41415° N, 86.55231° W

Did You Know? Between January 2015 and January 2018, all caves in the Hoosier National Forest were closed to prevent the spread of white-nose syndrome among federally protected bat species.

Rocky Hollow-Falls Canyon Nature Preserve

Located in Turkey Run State Park on the north side of Sugar Creek, this nature preserve is a narrow canyon surrounded by towering sandstone walls that serve as growing spots for native hemlock trees, ferns, and hydrangeas. The canyon is extremely shady because of the canopy of vegetation, so it offers a respite from the hot sun in the summer. At the head of the gorge, you'll find the numerous miniature waterfalls that give the canyon its name. Designated a national landmark in 1974, the 1,609-acre preserve has six hiking trails, the most rugged of which is Trail #3. This trail also provides the preserve's most interesting views, but there are deep gorges, wooden ladders, streams, and muddy inclines along the way.

Best Time to Visit: The best times to visit are during the fall for drier trails and the spring for fuller waterfalls.

Pass/Permit/Fees: There is a $7 fee for in-state vehicles and a $9 fee for out-of-state vehicles. There is also a $2 fee per person for walk-ins.

Closest City or Town: Bloomingdale

Physical Address: Cox Ford Road, Bloomingdale, IN 47832

GPS Coordinates: 39.89410° N, 87.20455° W

Did You Know? Fishing is allowed in Sugar Creek, where anglers can catch rock bass, flathead catfish, channel catfish, smallmouth bass, largemouth bass, and more.

Charles C. Deam Wilderness

The Charles C. Deam Wilderness is a dream for hikers, backpackers, and horseback riders. With 36 miles of varied-terrain trails available, you can explore this area for days without repeating a trek. Five trailheads with parking lots will get you started on your journey. Birdwatchers particularly enjoy the wilderness because there are scarlet tanagers, hawks, woodpeckers, red-eyed vireos, and flycatchers in the area. Since it's designated a wilderness, it is subject to special regulations that preserve its natural condition rather than turning it into a recreational area or park. For example, no wheeled vehicles, including bicycles and cars, are allowed in the wilderness. In addition, all mechanized equipment like generators is prohibited. You can also access Monroe Lake on the north side of the wilderness.

Best Time to Visit: Visit the Charles C. Deam Wilderness during the spring or fall when the weather is cooler.

Pass/Permit/Fees: There is no fee to visit the Charles C. Deam Wilderness unless you're riding a horse. There is a $5 fee for horseback riders.

Closest City or Town: Bloomington

Physical Address: Tower Ridge Road, Heltonville, IN 47436

GPS Coordinates: 39.03874° N, 86.35454° W

Did You Know? The Charles C. Deam Wilderness is named for the first Indiana state forester.

Monroe Lake

With 11,000 surface acres of water, Monroe Lake is the largest land-bound body of water in Indiana. The size of the lake makes it a popular destination for boating, fishing, and swimming (or just relaxing on the beach). Three public beaches around Monroe Lake are open between Memorial Day and Labor Day for swimming and beachside activities such as picnicking, volleyball, kite flying, frisbee, sandcastle building, sunbathing, and much more. The lake is a favorite of local fishermen because it boasts the most varied selection of fish in the county. Anglers regularly pull largemouth bass, yellow bass, bluegill, walleye, black crappie, white crappie, channel catfish, flathead catfish, bullhead stripers, and hybrid stripers from the water. Visitors can fish from the banks of Monroe Lake or from a boat directly on the lake. If you don't have your own boat, you can rent one here.

Best Time to Visit: Although fishing is available year round, visit during the summer for swimming.

Pass/Permit/Fees: There is no fee to visit Monroe Lake.

Closest City or Town: Bloomington

Physical Address: E. Monroe Dam Road, Bloomington, IN 47401

GPS Coordinates: 39.01170° N, 86.51053° W

Did You Know? Monroe Lake was built between 1960 and 1965 as a primary water source for Bloomington and to prevent flooding downstream.

Oliver Winery

What began as a hobby in the 1960s is now one of the largest wineries in the country. Oliver Winery was established by Indiana University law professor William Oliver, whose passion for making wine led him to turn his hobby into a winery located just northwest of Bloomington, Indiana. When his vines produced too many grapes for him to use on his own, he decided to expand it into a commercial operation. Oliver was heavily involved in helping pass the Indiana Small Winery Act in 1971, which allowed the creation of small wineries in the state. In 1983, Oliver's son Bill took over the winery and upgraded the guest experience by producing more varieties. By 1990, the winery was selling 25,000 cases per year.

Best Time to Visit: The tasting room is open Sunday through Thursday from 12:00 p.m. to 6:00 p.m. and Friday and Saturday from 11:00 a.m. to 8:00.

Pass/Permit/Fees: There is no fee to visit Oliver Winery, but you will need money to purchase tastings.

Closest City or Town: Bloomington

Physical Address: 200 E. Winery Road, Bloomington, IN 47404

GPS Coordinates: 39.28275° N, 86.52155° W

Did You Know? In 2017, Oliver Winery was named a top 25 winery to visit in the U.S. by *Travel + Leisure* magazine. It is also one of the 30 largest wineries in the country in addition to its best-in-class service and scenery.

Winzerwald Winery

An 85-acre winery owned by Dan and Donna Adams that's located in Hoosier National Forest, Winzerwald was established to a small degree in the 1800s by the founder's great-great-grandfather, Jakob Loesch. Loesch's grapes, which he brought with him to America from Germany, still grow in the area and are used to produce a limited-edition wine named Heirloom. These grapes have yet to be identified, but the Heirloom wine is the only product in the U.S. that uses them. The actual winery itself opened in 2002 and was expanded in 2018. The winery sticks close to its roots, producing wines made from grapes that are native to Germany, including Gewurztraminer, Pinot Meunier, and Riesling.

Best Time to Visit: The winery is open Tuesday through Sunday from 10:00 a.m. to 5:00 p.m. The restaurant is open from 11:30 a.m. to 4:30 p.m.

Pass/Permit/Fees: There is no fee to visit Winzerwald Winery, but be sure to bring money for tastings.

Closest City or Town: Bristow

Physical Address: 26300 North Indian Lake Road, Bristow, IN 47515

GPS Coordinates: 38.23010° N, 86.66213° W

Did You Know? *Winzerwald* is German for "vintner of the forest," which is an apt name for this winery in the forest. It reminded German settlers of the Black Forest in their home country.

Antique Alley

More than 1,200 antique dealers line the interlocking loop trails that make up Antique Alley, which has become one of the premier year-round antiquing destinations in the country. The trails take visitors through scenic eastern Indiana and past various historic locations. You'll find both large and small antique malls and shops, where an abundance of treasures await. Whether you're looking for furniture, farm tools, books, pottery, glassware, or collectibles, you're sure to find it in at least one of these shops. In historic Cambridge City, the center of Antique Alley, there are over 10 separate shops within a two-block area. If you're planning to visit every single shop, you'll definitely need several days to explore.

Best Time to Visit: This varies as each shop in Antique Alley sets its own hours.

Pass/Permit/Fees: There is no fee to visit Antique Alley, but if you plan to buy antiques, be sure to bring some money.

Closest City or Town: Cambridge City

Physical Address: W. Main Street, Cambridge City, IN 47327

GPS Coordinates: 39.81521° N, 85.17201° W

Did You Know? The Old National Road local to this area was once a main thoroughfare for horses and wagons. It connects Cambridge City, Centerville, and Richmond, among others.

Cave River Valley

This primitive nature preserve is an excellent place for true nature lovers to get out and explore the wilderness. There are streams, caves, ravines, and plenty of vegetation to provide a natural experience like no other. From the 1800s well into the 1900s, pioneers picnicked, fished, and took tours of River Cave. You'll even see the remains of mills and stills used to grind cornmeal or make whiskey and apple cider in years past. Be sure to take the ridge trail that passes by Bear Cave and ends at Lover's Leap, where you'll find a panoramic view of the entire valley. Afterward, you can tour the Endless Cave, which is a hibernation area for the endangered Indiana bat. You'll definitely catch a glimpse of them at dusk.

Best Time to Visit: The best time to visit Cave River Valley is during the spring or fall when the weather is cooler. Tours of the Endless Cave are scheduled only at certain times of the year. Check the website for dates.

Pass/Permit/Fees: There is no fee to visit Cave River Valley, but if you want a tour of Endless Cave, it is $15 per person.

Closest City or Town: Campbellsburg

Physical Address: 6031–6871 N. Cave River Valley Road, Campbellsburg, IN 47108

GPS Coordinates: 38.68847° N, 86.25808° W

Did You Know? The Endless Cave is 6,903 feet long.

Fossil Beds at Falls of the Ohio State Park

The fossil beds at the Falls of the Ohio State Park are among the largest exposed fossil beds in the world. The interpretive center located near the fossil beds provides interactive and immersive exhibits to tell the story of these fossils and the period in which the animals lived. Fossil collecting is prohibited at the park, but you are encouraged to explore the various types of fossils that are found only in sea beds from ancient waters. Guests can visit the collecting piles that contain fossils embedded in rock from quarries and can take home anything they find there.

Best Time to Visit: The interpretive center is open Monday through Saturday from 9:00 a.m. to 5:00 p.m. and Sunday from 1:00 p.m. to 5:00 p.m. The park is open daily from 7:00 a.m. to 11:00 p.m.

Pass/Permit/Fees: Admission is $9 for adults and $7 for children ages 5 to 11. Children under age five are free. There is also a $2 parking fee.

Closest City or Town: Clarksville

Physical Address: 201 W. Riverside Drive, Clarksville, IN 47129

GPS Coordinates: 38.27365° N, 85.76092° W

Did You Know? The fossil beds are 390 million years old. The rangers in the park will help you identify any fossils found in the collecting piles.

Indiana Cave Trail

The Indiana Cave Trail takes visitors into four commercial caves throughout the state: Bluespring Caverns, Marengo Cave, Indiana Caverns, and Squire Boone Caverns. While you can visit all four separately, the Cave Trail is an adventure that allows you to collect passport stamps for each one you visit and receive a T-shirt at the end of the trail. Each of the four caves is a unique system, so touring all of them will allow you to appreciate the differences in their formations. For instance, Marengo Caves is notable for its large rooms and abundant formations, and Bluespring Caverns is an underground river tour.

Best Time to Visit: Some caves are only open through October, and others are open year round. Check the website for details while planning your adventure.

Pass/Permit/Fees: Each cave has its own pricing. Check the website for rates.

Closest City or Town: Each cave is closest to a different town, but the most central town among the four caves is Corydon.

Physical Address: 1267 Green Acres Drive SW, Corydon, IN 47112

GPS Coordinates: 38.18401° N, 86.15213° W

Did You Know? Indiana Caverns, Indiana's longest cave system, is full of animal bones from the Ice Age.

Wellfield Botanic Gardens

At 36 acres in area, Wellfield Botanic Gardens is the perfect size for spending an afternoon immersed in a "living museum." The gardens are not only gorgeous and mesmerizing, but they also provide hydropower and drinking water to Elkhart residents. The Main Street Well, around which the gardens were developed, has been *a* source of drinking water for Elkhart since at least 1885 and *the* source since the early 1900s. The gardens were conceived as a community service project by the Rotary Club of Elkhart to celebrate the 100th anniversary of Rotary International. They were modeled after the Frederik Meijer Gardens & Sculpture Park in Michigan. The idea was to create an asset for the community that would attract tourists but also continue to serve the locals.

Best Time to Visit: The Wellfield Botanic Gardens are open daily from 10:00 a.m. to 6:00 p.m.

Pass/Permit/Fees: Admission is $8 for adults, $4 for children ages 3 to 12, and free for children under the age of 3.

Closest City or Town: Elkhart

Physical Address: 1011 N. Main Street, Elkhart, IN 46514

GPS Coordinates: 41.69704° N, 85.97678° W

Did You Know? There are more than 20 gardens at Wellfield Botanic Gardens, including a waterfall garden, a children's Adventure Path, and the Quilt Garden.

Hemlock Cliffs

Hemlock Cliffs is a box canyon in southern Indiana. It offers a cool climate, seasonal waterfalls, and sandstone rock formations, all of which combine to create the ideal environment for the rare trees and plants that grow here. Exploration of Hemlock Cliffs is encouraged, as there are rock outcrops, overhangs, rock shelters, ravines, small caves, springs, and other geological features throughout the area. Archaeological experts believe that Native Americans occupied this canyon as early as 10,000 years ago, and the large, semi-circular rock shelter at the head of the canyon likely provided them with shelter and defense. A 1-mile hiking trail will take you to the bottom of the canyon and past several waterfalls that only run in the spring. The trail can be challenging, particularly during the wet season, so take caution as you hike.

Best Time to Visit: The best time to visit Hemlock Cliffs is during the spring or summer after heavy rain when the waterfalls will be running.

Pass/Permit/Fees: There is no fee to visit Hemlock Cliffs.

Closest City or Town: English

Physical Address: National Forest Road, English, IN 47118

GPS Coordinates: 38.27819° N, 86.53824° W

Did You Know? The Hoosier National Forest is one of just three locations in the state where populations of wintergreen grow.

Angel Mounds State Historic Site

Constructed between 1000 CE and 1450 CE, the Angel Mounds State Historic Site is a well-preserved, pre-contact Native American town that was once occupied by approximately 1,000 Mississippian Native Americans. The earthen "angel" mounds were built to elevate buildings of significant importance. Twelve mounds scattered across 100 acres of land were built for residential and ceremonial purposes. Later, the site was a working farm that belonged to the Angel Family. In 1938, the land was purchased by the Indiana Historical Society to protect it, and an archaeological excavation began. Over 2.5 million artifacts were uncovered. These tell the story of the Mississippian culture, which was the first to build permanent communities and use agricultural techniques to work the land.

Best Time to Visit: The Angel Mounds State Historic Site is open Wednesday through Sunday from 10:00 a.m. to 5:00 p.m.

Pass/Permit/Fees: Admission is $8 for adults, $5 for children, and $7 for seniors.

Closest City or Town: Evansville

Physical Address: 8215 Pollack Avenue, Evansville, IN 47715

GPS Coordinates: 37.94607° N, 87.45180° W

Did You Know? The Mississippians left the site by 1450, though no one knows why.

Burdette Park

Burdette Park offers 170 acres of scenic area that provides education and entertainment for people of all ages. The Aquatic Center, which is open during the spring and summer, is one of the largest facilities of its kind in the Midwest. It offers an Olympic-size swimming pool with two diving boards, a family pool with two slides, a children's pool, and an interactive spray park. More adventurous visitors can enjoy a speed slide as well. At the O-Day Discovery Lodge, you can host corporate gatherings, weddings, large parties, and other events for up to 650 guests. A 3-mile paved trail is perfect for walking or biking, and several primitive trails are great for experienced hikers.

Best Time to Visit: Visit between Memorial Day and the second week of August if you want to go to the Aquatic Center. Otherwise, any time of the year is great.

Pass/Permit/Fees: Rates for the Aquatic Center are $8 for guests over age 12 and $5 for children ages 3 to 11 or seniors ages 62 and older. There is no fee to hike or fish in the park.

Closest City or Town: Evansville

Physical Address: 5301 Nurrenbern Road, Evansville, IN 47712

GPS Coordinates: 37.94279° N, 87.64014° W

Did You Know? The park opened in 1927 and the Aquatic Center opened in 1961.

Children's Museum of Evansville

Officially named the Koch Family Children's Museum of Evansville, this museum is designed to encourage children to explore, create, and discover through play. Three floors of activities and exhibits offer engaging educational material and sensory experiences to help children of all ages learn about science, math, literacy, culture, health, and the visual and performing arts. Originally called Hands On Discovery Children's Museum when it opened in 1990, the museum reopened in 2006 after closing for two years to complete a renovation and redesign of the exhibits. Until this new facility opened, there wasn't enough space to accommodate the huge interest in the museum. In fact, in 2004, more than 3,000 students representing 150 schools had to be turned away. This is no longer an issue with the expansive facility now in place.

Best Time to Visit: The museum is open Tuesday through Saturday from 9:00 a.m. to 4:00 p.m.

Pass/Permit/Fees: Admission is $10 per person for everyone ages 18 months of age and older.

Closest City or Town: Evansville

Physical Address: 22 SE 5th Street, Evansville, IN 47708

GPS Coordinates: 37.97212° N, 87.56931° W

Did You Know? Exhibits in the Children's Museum of Evansville include *Fantastic Place*, *Quack Factory*, *Work Smart*, and *Artmaker Studio*, among others.

Evansville Museum

In 1884, the Ladies' Literary Club began to encourage the study of art in Evansville, setting the stage for a successful art exhibition in 1900 that featured over 400 paintings, sculptures, historic books, war artifacts, and religious relics. The club began collecting art and artifacts to establish a permanent collection that became the cornerstone of the museum. The Barnes-Armstrong Historic Mansion was purchased as the home for the museum, which opened to the public in 1906. Over the following decades, the museum first moved to the former YWCA building when it merged with the Vanderburgh County Museum and Historical Society to become the Temple of Fine Arts in 1928, then to its own building (where it currently resides) in the 1950s.

Best Time to Visit: The museum is open Thursday through Saturday from 11:00 a.m. to 5:00 p.m. and Sunday from 12:00 p.m. to 5:00 p.m.

Pass/Permit/Fees: Admission is $12 for adults, $8 for children ages 4 to 17, and free for children under the age of 4.

Closest City or Town: Evansville

Physical Address: 411 SE Riverside Drive, Evansville, IN 47713

GPS Coordinates: 37.96559° N, 87.57253° W

Did You Know? The Evansville Museum houses 30,000 objects and sees 70,000 visitors each year.

Evansville Wartime Museum

The Evansville Wartime Museum is a fairly new addition to the city, having opened in 2017. The museum displays artifacts related to military history that have been donated by members of the community. It is dedicated to promoting awareness of Evansville's contributions to various military efforts. Located on the northwest corner of the Evansville Regional Airport grounds, the museum presents stories from the region's veterans and displays artifacts such as military vehicles, photos, aircraft, clothing, ammunition, posters, firearms, and more. There is also a memorial to all Evansville-area veterans who died in war, dating from the Civil War through Operation Iraqi Freedom.

Best Time to Visit: The museum is open Thursday through Sunday from 12:00 p.m. to 4:00 p.m.

Pass/Permit/Fees: Admission is $11 per person ($10 admission plus $1 service fee) for all patrons over the age of 5. Children ages 5 and under are free.

Closest City or Town: Evansville

Physical Address: 7503 Petersburg Road, Evansville, IN 47725

GPS Coordinates: 38.04260° N, 87.53763° W

Did You Know? Temporary exhibits such as *D-Day Revisited* and *47 On Display* travel to the museum, so no two visits will ever be the same.

Hartman Arboretum

Founded in 2001, the Hartman Arboretum is a natural preserve that allows people of all ages to learn about the diversity of trees and shrubs in southern Indiana. The arboretum features approximately 500 trees of all types, including 18 varieties of oak and 17 varieties of Redbud cultivar. The Wildlife Garden is a particular point of interest because it was planned by master gardeners. It provides host plants and nectar for various butterflies that call the arboretum home. Other areas to explore include a hydrangea collection, a "stumpery" woodland garden, a wall of crabapples, groves of young oaks, a wild meadow, a shrub collection, a memorial garden, a blueberry patch, and more.

Best Time to Visit: The best time to visit Hartman Arboretum is in the spring to see the trees in bloom or in the fall when you can see the changing colors of the foliage and the butterflies.

Pass/Permit/Fees: There is no fee to visit the Hartman Arboretum.

Closest City or Town: Evansville

Physical Address: 5939 Spirit Trail, Evansville, IN 47720

GPS Coordinates: 38.03013° N, 87.64819° W

Did You Know? A large number of the trees and shrubs in the Hartman Arboretum are native to southern Indiana, western Kentucky, southern Illinois, or the Shawnee Hills area.

Howell Wetlands

One of just five urban wetland parks in Indiana, Howell Wetlands features 35 acres of marshland, oxbow lake, bald cypress slough, upland meadow, and lowland hardwood forest, along with the wildlife that calls these habitats home. Expect to see animals such as deer, muskrats, beavers, wood ducks, geese, and herons during your visit. Walking trails and boardwalks throughout the park allow visitors to experience these diverse ecosystems. The park also offers plenty of recreational opportunities, including basketball, miniature golf, a par-3 golf course, and a swimming pool. The Ohio River once flowed through this area and regularly spilled floodwaters over its banks, creating the wetlands.

Best Time to Visit: The best time to visit the Howell Wetlands is during the fall, when migratory birds are stopping in the area on their way south and the leaves are changing colors.

Pass/Permit/Fees: There is no fee to visit the Howell Wetlands.

Closest City or Town: Evansville

Physical Address: 1400 S. Tekoppel Avenue, Evansville, IN 47712

GPS Coordinates: 37.96240° N, 87.61872° W

Did You Know? The city of Evansville officially declared the area a wetland in 1997 to conserve the habitats and provide community educational opportunities.

Isaac Knight Memorial

When 13-year-old Isaac Knight was playing with a group of boys by the Ohio River in 1793, the Potawatomi and Kickapoo Native American tribes took the group by surprise, killed two of them, and kidnapped the other three. Knight managed to escape his captors two and a half years later and went in search of his family, who believed Isaac to be dead and had moved to another area during his ordeal. He eventually located them in 1795, and they were reunited. The memorial that stands on Lincoln Avenue today marks Knight's original grave site. It was established in 1974 by his great-great-granddaughter, Louise Fairchild Van Buskirk. Knight eventually published a book that detailed his capture, escape, and arduous journey to find his family.

Best Time to Visit: The best time to visit the Isaac Knight Memorial is during the spring or fall when the weather is cooler.

Pass/Permit/Fees: There is no fee to visit the Isaac Knight Memorial.

Closest City or Town: Evansville

Physical Address: 556 S. Green River Road, Evansville, IN 47715

GPS Coordinates: 37.9697° N, 87.4921° W

Did You Know? As an adult, Isaac Knight moved to Vanderburgh County to make his home. Eventually, Knight Township would be named for this early historical figure.

Reitz Home Museum

As the only Victorian House Museum in Evansville, the Reitz Home Museum is a must-see stop for anyone visiting the city. It's located in the downtown Historic Preservation District. The house was completed in 1871 for German immigrant John Augustus Reitz, who came to the United States in the 1930s along with millions of other Germans looking for business opportunities and a hands-off government. By the 1880s, Reitz's sawmill on Pigeon Creek was producing more hardwood lumber than any other mill in the U.S. The house was donated to the Daughters of Isabella in 1934 and sold to the Evansville Diocese in 1945. Finally, it was purchased by the Evansville Junior League for preservation in 1974.

Best Time to Visit: The Reitz Home Museum is open Tuesday through Saturday from 11:00 a.m. to 2:30 p.m. in the summer. It's closed on Friday as well from January through March.

Pass/Permit/Fees: Admission is $7.50 for adults, $1.50 for children ages 12 and under, and $2.50 for students.

Closest City or Town: Evansville

Physical Address: 112 Chestnut Street, Evansville, IN 47713

GPS Coordinates: 37.96831° N, 87.57229° W

Did You Know? It has been called one of the best examples of French Second Empire architecture in the country.

USS LST-325

The USS *LST-325*, the only remaining operational WWII Landing Ship Tank in the U.S., is open for tours throughout the year and sails along the inland rivers in early fall. The ship was commissioned in 1943 and placed under the command of Ensign Clifford E. Mosier, who commanded the ship until 1945. In 1944, *LST-325* was part of the backup force for the soldiers who stormed Omaha Beach on D-Day. Between June 1944 and April 1945, the ship made 43 round trips between France and England, dropping off troops at Omaha, Utah, Gold, and Juno beaches as well as the city of Rouen on the Seine River.

Best Time to Visit: The ship is open for tours from April through November on Sunday from 12:00 p.m. to 4:00 p.m. and Tuesday through Saturday from 10:00 a.m. to 4:00 p.m.

Pass/Permit/Fees: Admission is $15 for adults, $7.50 for children ages 6 to 17, and free for children under the age of 6.

Closest City or Town: Evansville

Physical Address: 610 NW Riverside Drive, Evansville, IN 47708

GPS Coordinates: 37.97394° N, 87.58025° W

Did You Know? In December 1944, the ship helped rescue 700 soldiers from the S.S. *Empire Javelin*, which had been hit by a torpedo off the coast of France.

Willard Carpenter House

Now a memorial to Evansville philanthropist Willard Carpenter, this two-story Greek Revival–style mansion was built by carpenter Gottlieb Bippus and masons Tenford and Knoll between 1848 and 1849. At the time, the Willard Carpenter House was a conspicuous mansion that drew people in from miles around to see it.

During the Depression, the house was purchased by Funkhouser American Legion Post. It was sold in 1956 to WTVW before being acquired by Medco in 1974 to be restored to its original form. Medco occupied the residence until 1985, when it was purchased by WNIN television to house the offices of the TV channel and its FM radio affiliate.

Best Time to Visit: The Willard Carpenter House can be enjoyed any time of the year.

Pass/Permit/Fees: There is no fee to visit the Willard Carpenter House.

Closest City or Town: Evansville

Physical Address: 413 Carpenter Street, Evansville, IN 47708

GPS Coordinates: 37.97581° N, 87.57568° W

Did You Know? Currently, the Willard Carpenter House stands vacant, but it's still a sight to see from the road.

Conner Prairie Interactive History Park

Established by Eli Lilly in 1934, Connor Prairie Interactive History Park is a unique destination that offers hands-on, individualized, and engaging experiences that combine history with science to explore Indiana's natural and cultural heritage. Several historically themed experience areas are located across the 800-acre wooded property.

Some of these experiences include the *Makesmith Workshop*, *Animal Encounters*, *1836 Prairietown*, *Lenape Indian Camp*, *the William Conner House*, *1863 Civil War Journey*, *1859 Balloon Voyage*, *Discovery Station* and *Craft Corner*, and the *Treetop Outpost*.

Best Time to Visit: The park is open April 30 through November 3, Tuesday through Sunday, from 10:00 a.m. to 5:00 p.m.

Pass/Permit/Fees: Admission is $18 for adults, $13 for children ages 2 to 12, and $17 for seniors. Children under the age of 2 are free.

Closest City or Town: Fishers

Physical Address: 13400 Allisonville Road, Fishers, IN 46038

GPS Coordinates: 39.98550° N, 86.02869° W

Did You Know? Conner Prairie Interactive History Park was recently designated a Site of Conscience because it connects past struggles to current human rights movements.

K1 Speed

If you're an automobile-racing enthusiast and dream about careening around the Indianapolis Motor Speedway, you definitely want to visit K1 Speed, where you can experience the rush of racing the Indy 500, although on a smaller scale. The facility's all-electric go-karts are faster and easier to drive than their gas-powered rivals. Once you're done driving, you can enjoy the numerous arcade games and air hockey tables or catch a bite to eat at the Paddock Lounge. K1 Speed prides itself on being a world-class entertainment center that provides an authentic racing environment. Even the most experienced go-kart drivers will get a thrill from racing on the professionally designed track.

Best Time to Visit: K1 Speed is open Monday through Thursday from 12:00 p.m. to 10:00 p.m., Friday from 12:00 p.m. to 12:00 a.m., Saturday from 10:00 a.m. to 12:00 p.m., and Sunday from 10:00 a.m. to 10:00 p.m.

Pass/Permit/Fees: Races start at $23.95 for a single race. Discounts apply for more races on the same day.

Closest City or Town: Fishers

Physical Address: 9998 E. 121st Street, Fishers, IN 46037

GPS Coordinates: 39.96746° N, 85.99085° W

Did You Know? The indoor go-karting experience at K1 Speed features one of the longest straightaways of any indoor karting facility, making passing a fun and exciting challenge.

Mesker Park Zoo and Botanic Garden

Evansville business leader Gilmore M. Haynie founded the Mesker Park Zoo and Botanic Garden in 1928 with just two lion cubs, an elephant, and several antelope. Between then and 2008, when the zoo underwent a major expansion, more than 150 animals moved into their exhibits.

The Mesker Park Zoo was one of the first facilities to use a moat system to keep visitors a safe distance from the animals and still display them in the most natural habitat possible. The zoo is now home to jaguars, Mexican gray wolves, red pandas, clouded leopards, lemurs, giraffes, camels, Amur tigers, and many more.

Best Time to Visit: The zoo is open daily from 9:00 a.m. to 4:00 p.m.

Pass/Permit/Fees: Between March and October, admission is $9.50 for adults and $8.50 for children ages 3 to 12. Between November and February, admission is $7.50 for adults and $6.50 for children ages 3 to 12. Children under age 3 are always free.

Closest City or Town: Evansville

Physical Address: 1545 Mesker Park Drive, Evansville, IN 47720

GPS Coordinates: 37.99715° N, 87.60615 W

Did You Know? Numerous botanical gardens throughout Mesker Park are designed both for visitor enjoyment and animal consumption.

African/African-American Historical Museum

The African/African-American Historical Museum has the largest public collection of African Art in Fort Wayne. The tour starts with an introduction to the Middle Passage, the route that millions of Africans traveled when they were shipped to the Western Hemisphere as part of the Atlantic slave trade. Drawings and photos show how slaves lived aboard the ships at that time, and there's a Senufu bird sculpture that represented hope to the slaves who were forced to leave their homeland. In the *Pre-Colonial African Arts Exhibit*, visitors can see a sculpture from each region of Africa from Executive Director Dr. John Aden's personal collection. Other rooms are dedicated to African women, music, community roles, and the *Black Wings American Dreams of Flight* exhibit. The museum's goal is to highlight the stories of Africans in Allen County.

Best Time to Visit: It is open by appointment only.

Pass/Permit/Fees: Admission is $7 for adults and $5 for children.

Closest City or Town: Fort Wayne

Physical Address: 426 E. Douglas Avenue, Fort Wayne, IN 46802

GPS Coordinates: 41.11251° N, 85.14134° W

Did You Know? The acronym for the African/African-American Historical Museum (AAAHM) is pronounced "awesome."

Allen County War Memorial Coliseum

Constructed as a memorial to veterans of all U.S. wars, the Allen County War Memorial Coliseum is a multi-purpose arena that opened in 1953. It was originally meant to be a facility for hockey and basketball games, seating 8,103 for the former and 10,240 for the latter. In 1989, a 108,000-square-foot Exposition Center was added to host trade shows and other events. This included another 7,500 seats. A $35 million renovation in 2002 raised the roof of the coliseum by 41 feet and increased the capacity to 10,500 for hockey and 13,000 for basketball. Currently, the coliseum is home to the Fort Wayne Komets hockey team, the Fort Wayne Mad Ants basketball team, and the Fort Wayne Derby Girls flat-track derby team.

Best Time to Visit: Visit the memorial during basketball and hockey season (late fall to late spring).

Pass/Permit/Fees: The fee to visit the Allen County War Memorial Coliseum depends on the event and seat selection.

Closest City or Town: Fort Wayne

Physical Address: 4000 Parnell Avenue, Fort Wayne, IN 46805

GPS Coordinates: 41.11639° N, 85.12413° W

Did You Know? The Allen County War Memorial Coliseum has hosted numerous large events, including the 1955 and 1956 NBA Finals, the 1953 NBA All-Star Game, and the annual Rumble in Fort Wayne midget car race.

Arena Dinner Theatre

Originally known as Fort Wayne Theatre Workshop, the Arena Dinner Theatre got its start because of Fort Wayne Parks Department budget cuts in 1974. This was the only theatre in town that was performing in the round. When its funding was eliminated, the board had to find a new way to keep community theatre alive in Fort Wayne. The board members conceived of a dinner theatre to be held in the Fort Wayne Chamber Building's Anthony Wayne Ballroom. This arrangement lasted for 10 years, then the theatre changed directions again and became a traveling troupe before finding a permanent home in the building that formerly housed the Fort Wayne Art School Little Theater. The 112-seat facility now offers seven shows each year and serves dinner from the kitchen located on the premises.

Best Time to Visit: The Arena Dinner Theatre's season runs from October through June.

Pass/Permit/Fees: The fee to visit the Arena Dinner Theatre depends on show and seat selection.

Closest City or Town: Fort Wayne

Physical Address: 719 Rockhill Street, Fort Wayne, IN 46802

GPS Coordinates: 41.07815° N, 85.15361° W

Did You Know? No seat in the Arena Dinner Theatre is more than 30 feet from the stage, making productions extremely intimate. Several theatre workshops are offered to actors and directors throughout the year.

Cathedral of the Immaculate Conception

The Cathedral of the Immaculate Conception Catholic Church was established in 1836 under the name St. Mary's Church, making it the oldest church in Fort Wayne. In 1840, a new church, the Cathedral of St. Augustine, replaced St. Mary's and stood until it was destroyed by fire in 1859.

A third church, now named the Cathedral of the Immaculate Conception, was built between 1859 and 1860; that is the structure that stands today. It is located on Cathedral Square, and the Cathedral Museum is just a few blocks' walk from the actual church. In 1980, the cathedral was listed on the National Register of Historic Places.

Best Time to Visit: If you want to see the Cathedral of the Immaculate Conception during Mass, visit on Saturday at 5:00 p.m.; Sunday at 8:30 a.m., 11:30 a.m., or 5:00 p.m.; Monday through Friday at 8:00 a.m. or 12:05 p.m.; and the first Friday of each month at 7:00 a.m.

Pass/Permit/Fees: There is no fee to visit the cathedral.

Closest City or Town: Fort Wayne

Physical Address: 1122 S. Clinton Street, Fort Wayne, IN 46802

GPS Coordinates: 41.07637° N, 85.13810° W

Did You Know? The stained glass windows that depict various scenes in Mary's life were created in Munich, Germany. They were installed in the cathedral in 1896.

DeBrand Fine Chocolates

DeBrand Fine Chocolates opened in October 1987, the culmination of the dream of founder Cathy Brand-Beere, who began working with chocolate at age 8. Throughout her childhood and teenage years, Brand-Beere sold chocolate candy and custom-designed wedding cakes to her friends and family members. However, her ultimate goal was realized when she opened her own "real" chocolate shop in Fort Wayne. Now the chocolate company has four retail outlets in Fort Wayne and one in Indianapolis. Brand-Beere only uses the highest-quality ingredients, whether they're imported or locally sourced from Indiana producers.

Best Time to Visit: The headquarters chocolate shop is open Monday through Thursday from 7:00 a.m. to 9:00 p.m., Friday from 7:00 a.m. to 10:00 p.m., Saturday from 10:00 a.m. to 10:00 p.m., and Sunday from 12:00 p.m. to 6:00 p.m. Tours are available Tuesday at 10:00 a.m., Thursday at 1:00 p.m., and Saturday at 10:30 a.m.

Pass/Permit/Fees: Tours are $10 per person, but guests also receive $10 off a purchase of $20 or more.

Closest City or Town: Fort Wayne

Physical Address: 5608 Coldwater Road, Fort Wayne, IN 46825

GPS Coordinates: 41.17585° N, 85.11520° W

Did You Know? The DeBrand name came from the French prefix *De-* and the last name Brand. It means "from Brand."

Eagle Marsh Nature Preserve

This 831-acre wetland preserve features over 14 miles of trails for hikers to enjoy shallow-water wetland, prairie, sedge meadow, and mature forest habitats. While visiting the preserve, you can see many of the 250 species of birds and other wild animals that call the preserve home. Several of these species are on the endangered list or are of special concern in the state. You may even glimpse a bald eagle or two because at least one pair has raised eaglets in the area. Eagle Marsh opened in 2005 and has since added land to increase the habitat available for various birds and animals, particularly those that live in a mature forest habitat. In 2019, Eagle Marsh expanded by another 75 acres to include a section of heavily wooded land that has been undisturbed since at least 1938.

Best Time to Visit: The best time to visit is during the spring or fall when the temperatures are mild.

Pass/Permit/Fees: There is no fee to visit the Eagle Marsh Nature Preserve, but donations are appreciated.

Closest City or Town: Fort Wayne

Physical Address: 6801 Engle Road, Fort Wayne, IN 46804

GPS Coordinates: 41. 03793° N, 85.22670° W

Did You Know? The Arrowhead Prairie at Eagle Marsh represents the original tallgrass prairie land that once covered most of Indiana. More than 98 percent of those grasslands have been destroyed.

Foellinger-Freimann Botanical Conservatory

Two friends, Helene Foellinger and Bill Sowers, wanted to provide an indoor nature sanctuary for the community to enjoy year round. Foellinger and Sowers often traveled the world together, enjoying gardens and other botanical wonders, and they wanted to share the beauty they experienced with their fellow Fort Wayne residents. They decided to raise funds to establish their dream with the Foellinger-Freimann Botanical Conservatory. They received significant financial backing from the Foellinger Foundation and the Freimann Trust, thus providing the name of the facility. It is operated by the Fort Wayne Parks and Recreation Department and provides a natural escape for thousands of visitors each year.

Best Time to Visit: You can enjoy the conservatory any time of the year.

Pass/Permit/Fees: The conservatory is open Tuesday, Wednesday, and Saturday from 10:00 a.m. to 5:00 p.m., Thursday from 10:00 a.m. to 8:00 p.m., and Sunday from 12:00 p.m. to 4:00 p.m.

Closest City or Town: Fort Wayne

Physical Address: 1100 S. Calhoun Street, Fort Wayne, IN 46802

GPS Coordinates: 41.07637° N, 85.13915° W

Did You Know? The conservatory has 24,500 square feet of indoor gardens that change four times a year.

44

Foellinger Theatre

This outdoor theatre provides informal open-air concerts. Located in Franke Park, the theatre is used primarily for a summer concert and movie series. The stage and audience seats were built into a grassy hillside. The theatre, which has a capacity of 2,751 guests, can be rented for special events like lectures, community theater or concert performances, religious services, and other large gatherings. Top musical acts such as Air Supply, Incubus, Dire Straits, Pixies, REO Speedwagon, Bachman Cummings, and many more make a stop at Foellinger Theatre due to its superior acoustics and scenic environment. Constructed in 1949, the theatre was a gift from Helene Foellinger in memory of her father, Oscar G. Foellinger. Mr. Foellinger was the formal publisher of the *Fort Wayne News-Sentinel*.

Best Time to Visit: The best time to visit Foellinger Theatre is during the summer concert season.

Pass/Permit/Fees: Ticket costs for concerts will vary. Movie nights on Wednesday are free to the community.

Closest City or Town: Fort Wayne

Physical Address: 3411 Sherman Boulevard, Fort Wayne, IN 46808

GPS Coordinates: 41.10508° N, 85.15610° W

Did You Know? More than 50,000 people attend concerts, movies, and other events at the Foellinger Theatre every year.

Fort Wayne Aviation Museum

Located at Fort Wayne International Airport, this museum opened in 1984 and was recently moved from an area beyond airport security to an unsecured section of the terminal to allow for better accessibility to patrons other than ticketed passengers. The museum is home to artifacts that tell the stories of aviation pioneers like World War I ace pilot Paul Baer, Woman's Airforce Service Pilot (WASP) Margaret Ringenberg, and daredevil Art "The Bird Boy" Smith, all of whom have ties to Fort Wayne.

In addition, the museum now offers digital exhibits that tell the story of aviation in Fort Wayne. A 24-foot wall with numerous displays presents an aviation timeline that gives visitors an audio history of local aviation. An augmented-reality attraction allows visitors to fly with Ringenberg, tour the control tower, or pilot Art Smith's 1911 airplane.

Best Time to Visit: The museum is open 24/7.

Pass/Permit/Fees: There is no fee to visit Fort Wayne Aviation Museum.

Closest City or Town: Fort Wayne

Physical Address: 3801 W. Ferguson Road, Fort Wayne, IN 46809

GPS Coordinates: 40.98725° N, 85.18819° W

Did You Know? Most of the museum's 3,000-item collection is now housed at the History Center since this experience has transitioned to a digital one.

Fort Wayne Children's Zoo

This nationally ranked zoo offers 40 acres of animals, gorgeous landscapes, and exhilarating rides. In the African Journey, you can see lions, monkeys, hyenas, and zebras; ride the Sky Safari; or enjoy interactive experiences such as feeding giraffes. In the Australian Adventure, you can pet a stingray, explore the outback, or ride a surfboard. You can even take a canoe down the river on the Crocodile Creek Adventure Ride. In the Indonesian Rainforest, visit Dr. Diversity's Research Station and climb the Tree Top Trail or relax and ride the Endangered Species Carousel to learn about animals that need protection. Visit the Central Zoo to pet a goat at the Indiana Family Farm, watch the sea lions at feeding time, or stroll through Monkey Island.

Best Time to Visit: The zoo is open daily, May through August, from 9:00 a.m. to 7:00 p.m. and in April, September, and October from 9:00 a.m. to 5:00 p.m.

Pass/Permit/Fees: Admission is $15 for adults, $11 for children ages 2 to 18, $13 for seniors, and free for children under age 2.

Closest City or Town: Fort Wayne

Physical Address: 3411 Sherman Boulevard, Fort Wayne, IN 46808

GPS Coordinates: 41.10653° N, 85.15361° W

Did You Know? The zoo's roots date back to 1952 when a 54-acre nature preserve was added to Franke Park.

Fort Wayne Firefighters Museum

In 1974, two years after Fire Station #3 in downtown Fort Wayne was closed by the city, the Fort Wayne Firefighters Museum was established. This nonprofit organization began renovating the fire station and opened the museum on a limited basis in 1981. The group continued renovations and was eventually deeded the property in 1987. In 1998, 2009, and 2019, the exhibit space was expanded as an ever-growing collection of artifacts went on display.

The museum established regular hours in 2001 and began teaching fire safety workshops to visitors of all ages. Currently, two floors of exhibits feature historic items such as various types of firefighting equipment and photos.

Best Time to Visit: The museum is open Monday, Tuesday, Thursday, and Friday from 10:00 a.m. to 4:00 p.m. and on Saturday from 10:00 a.m. to 3:00 p.m.

Pass/Permit/Fees: Admission is $4 for adults, $3 for seniors ages 60 and older, and $3 for students ages 6 to 12.

Closest City or Town: Fort Wayne

Physical Address: 226 W. Washington Boulevard, Fort Wayne, IN 46802

GPS Coordinates: 41.07762° N, 85.14194° W

Did You Know? Engine House #3 was built in 1893 and employed six firefighters. It owned four horses, a chemical wagon, and a hose wagon.

Fort Wayne Museum of Art

The Fort Wayne Museum of Art originated in 1888 as an art school that offered informal classes in painting and drawing. Eventually, these classes were formalized under the name of the Fort Wayne Art School. In 1921, a museum component was added to the art school when ten paintings were donated by a prominent Fort Wayne resident, Theodore Thieme. Twenty-eight years later, Thieme also donated his residence to the school, and it became the facility that housed art exhibits and collections. In 1977, the museum and art school separated when the school became a part of Indiana University at Fort Wayne. The museum moved to a new facility in 1984, where it still resides today.

Best Time to Visit: The museum is open Tuesday, Wednesday, Friday, and Saturday from 10:00 a.m. to 6:00 p.m., Thursday from 10:00 a.m. to 8:00 p.m., and Sunday from 12:00 p.m. to 5:00 p.m.

Pass/Permit/Fees: Admission is $8 for adults and $6 for seniors ages 65 and up. General admission is free on Thursday from 5:00 p.m. to 8:00 p.m.

Closest City or Town: Fort Wayne

Physical Address: 311 E. Main Street, Fort Wayne, IN 46802

GPS Coordinates: 41.08201° N, 85.13601° W

Did You Know? The Fort Wayne Museum of Art has a collection of approximately 5,000 American sculptures, drawings, paintings, prints, and more.

Headwaters Park

In Fort Wayne, there are few places better than Headwaters Park for a festival, concert, or charity event. The large open-air pavilion can be rented for receptions, picnics, family reunions, and company parties. In the winter, the Headwaters Ice Skating Rink is ideal for exercise and competition.

Established in the 1990s, the park was designed to provide an educational experience to visitors as well as a place for recreation. The trees, flowers, and grasses were all selected for their diversity so that young people could learn about them. The interactive water fountain provides a respite from the heat in the summer and is a showpiece of art during other seasons. The park was fully completed in 2008 with the addition of the Madge Rothschild Pavilion and is now a community gathering place for events and leisure.

Best Time to Visit: Visit Headwaters Park during the summer for the fountain and the winter for the skating rink.

Pass/Permit/Fees: There is no fee to visit the park.

Closest City or Town: Fort Wayne

Physical Address: 333 S. Clinton Street, Fort Wayne, IN 46802

GPS Coordinates: 41.08577° N, 85.13911° W

Did You Know? More than 400,000 people have skated on the ice at the Headwaters Ice Skating Rink in the 17 years since it opened.

Lakeside Park & Rose Garden

Designed by Parks Adolf Jaenicke in 1920, the sunken rose garden design was conceived out of a need to turn a 6-foot-deep depression used as a dump into a visually stunning landmark. It was assumed that the state's harsh winters would prohibit the growth of roses until Jaenicke discovered that the Indiana clay provided an ideal environment for them. The resulting sunken gardens and reflecting ponds that have brought thousands of guests to Lakeside Park proved him right. In 2005, the gardens were renovated to replace the stairs, retaining walls, reflecting pools, and sidewalks, which had fallen into disrepair. The reconstruction team took efforts to retain the original design while making the facilities more durable. Increased lighting, a bronze fountain, and other improvements only added to the park's pleasant surroundings.

Best Time to Visit: The best time to visit Lakeside Park & Rose Garden is during the early summer when the roses are in bloom.

Pass/Permit/Fees: There is no fee to visit.

Closest City or Town: Fort Wayne

Physical Address: 1401 Lake Avenue, Fort Wayne, IN 46805

GPS Coordinates: 41.09015° N, 85.11784° W

Did You Know? The rose garden, which was designated a National Rose Garden in 1928, boasts over 2,000 rose plants of more than 150 varieties.

Mad Anthony Brewing Company

Founded in 1998 by Todd Grantham and Blaine Stuckey, Mad Anthony Brewing Company brews over 2,500 barrels of beer each year. The company has the distinction of being the first microbrewery in Indianapolis, which has led to its popularity among thousands of local and regional customers. No matter what's on tap, from the company's Good Karma IPA to its seasonal Snowplowed Winter Ale, there's sure to be a beer for everyone, regardless of their personal preferences. Jeff Neels, director of restaurant operations, serves delicious food like chicken and waffles, blackened whitefish po' boys, gourmet pizza, buffalo cauliflower bites, and more to pair with the specialty beers brewed on site.

Best Time to Visit: Mad Anthony Brewing Company is open Sunday, Monday, Wednesday, and Thursday from 11:00 a.m. to 10:00 p.m. and Friday and Saturday from 11:00 a.m. to 11:00 p.m. It is closed on Tuesday.

Pass/Permit/Fees: There is no fee to visit.

Closest City or Town: Fort Wayne

Physical Address: 2002 Broadway, Fort Wayne, IN 46802

GPS Coordinates: 41.06811° N, 85.15284° W

Did You Know? Mad Anthony Brewing Company is located in the building that used to house the first Kroger store in Fort Wayne. However, the space was better known as the Munchie Emporium restaurant, which is now the brewery's family dining room.

Native Trees of Indiana River Walk

Presented by Purdue Fort Wayne University, the Native Trees of Indiana River Walk is a project designed to sustain the ecology of the St. Joseph River. Root systems of various trees planted adjacent to the river have stabilized the banks to help prevent soil erosion. It is also a way for visitors to become familiar with trees that are hard to find in urban environments. Along the 1.25-mile path, you'll discover over 100 trees that are native to Indiana.

The eight-foot-wide paved trail allows people of all ages and abilities to view live specimens of native plants in their natural setting. You may also spot wildlife and other interesting plants, including fruit, flowers, and bushes. The trailhead is located near Parking Lot 10, which is east of the St. Joseph River on the Purdue Fort Wayne campus.

Best Time to Visit: Visit the Native Trees of Indiana River Walk during the fall when the leaves are changing colors.

Pass/Permit/Fees: There is no fee to visit the Native Trees of Indiana River Walk.

Closest City or Town: Fort Wayne

Physical Address: 2 5N, Fort Wayne, IN 46815

GPS Coordinates: 41.45763° N, 85.21327° W

Did You Know? Some trees you'll see on the Native Trees Indiana River Walk include buckeyes, ash, bald cypress, black maples, hawthorns, crabapples, and pawpaws. You can even take any fruit from the trees that you find.

Old Fort Wayne

Built by Major John Whistler and his soldiers between 1815 and 1816, Old Fort Wayne was the last of three American forts to be constructed at the confluence of the Maumee, St. Mary's, and St. Joseph rivers. The fort was designed to allow a small band of between 50 and 75 soldiers to easily defend themselves from a Native American attack. It included two picket lines, heave gates, and blockhouses. At the time, it was the most complex all-wooden fort ever built in North America, but it was abandoned just three years after construction because of the rapid westward movement of the frontier. This replica of the original fort opened to the public for tours and events on July 4, 1976.

Best Time to Visit: The fort is only open in the summer, Wednesday through Saturday from 10:00 a.m. to 5:00 p.m. and Sunday from 12:00 p.m. to 4:00 p.m.

Pass/Permit/Fees: There is no fee to visit Old Fort Wayne, but some activities may require a separate fee.

Closest City or Town: Fort Wayne, Indiana

Physical Address: 1201 Spy Run Avenue, Fort Wayne, IN 46805

GPS Coordinates: 42.30112° N, 83.09810° W

Did You Know? Depending on when you visit Old Fort Wayne, you'll see a different era represented, ranging from the early 1600s through World War II. Check the website for specific events.

Parkview Field

Parkview Field is the baseball home of the Fort Wayne TinCaps, the High-A Central affiliate of the San Diego Padres. It opened on April 16, 2009 as a replacement for Memorial Stadium, the team's former home. Parkview Field is named for Parkview Health, which bought the naming rights for a term of 10 years for $3 million. Current capacity is 6,156 fans in fixed seats and 8,100 fans with temporary seating. There are 16 luxury suites, the Appleseed Picnic Pavilion in right field, the Treetops Rooftop Party Area, and Home Run Porch in left field. The park also has lawn seating and an $800,000 private-investment suite located in the "batter's eye" section of the field. (This is usually left empty because it can distract the batter.)

Best Time to Visit: Visit Parkview Field during baseball season in late spring, summer, and early fall.

Pass/Permit/Fees: The fee to visit Parkview Field depends on game and seat selection.

Closest City or Town: Fort Wayne

Physical Address: 1301 Ewing Street, Fort Wayne, IN 46802

GPS Coordinates: 41.07502° N, 85.14277° W

Did You Know? *Baseball Digest* named Parkview Field "Ballpark of the Year" in 2009 and *Stadium Journey* magazine called it the "Top Minor League Baseball Experience" in 2011, 2012, 2014, and 2015.

Rivergreenway Trail

Located in Fort Wayne, the Rivergreenway Trail is a 25-mile linear park that traces the St. Mary's, St. Joseph, and Maumee rivers. It is a popular park for recreation and fitness because it's ideal for hiking, jogging, bicycling, rollerblading, and walking. Many people find it an excellent place for nature study as well because it offers a variety of vegetation, scenic views, and the occasional opportunity to see wildlife.

The three main pathways, one for each river, collectively run through neighborhoods, past historical attractions, and into 15 city parks. Since portions of the trails are directly adjacent to the rivers, they can be flooded at times, so be sure to check for updates on the website after heavy rains.

Best Time to Visit: The best time to visit the trail is during spring or fall when the weather is mild.

Pass/Permit/Fees: There is no fee to visit the trail.

Closest City or Town: Fort Wayne

Physical Address: St. Mary's Pathway, Fort Wayne, IN 46805

GPS Coordinates: 41. 08485° N, 85.13429° W

Did You Know? The Rivergreenway Trail is a wonderful way to explore the natural side of Fort Wayne and visit local sites such as the Historic Old Fort, Hosey Dam, the Indiana University-Purdue University Fort Wayne campus, downtown Fort Wayne, and city parks such as Shoaff Park.

Science Central

More than 200 permanent interactive science exhibits and touring displays await visitors at Science Central, a hands-on science museum for people of all ages. Activities include sliding down a 2-story slide, viewing a mastodon that was discovered in Allen County, walking on the moon, and participating in a live science experiment. There are exhibits on everything from magnets, sound, and light to optical illusions, live animals, and liquid nitrogen. You may need more than a day at Science Central to experience everything the museum has to offer. The center is located in the 1908 building that once housed City Light & Power, Fort Wayne's first publicly run electric utility. In 1975, the power plant closed, and the building sat vacant for 16 years before it was renovated for the science museum.

Best Time to Visit: Science Central is open Thursday and Friday from 10:00 a.m. to 4:00 p.m., Saturday from 10:00 a.m. to 5:00 p.m., and Sunday from 12:00 p.m. to 5:00 p.m.

Pass/Permit/Fees: Admission is $10 per person for visitors ages 3 and up.

Closest City or Town: Fort Wayne

Physical Address: 1950 N. Clinton Street, Fort Wayne, IN 46805

GPS Coordinates: 41.09237° N, 85.13932° W

Did You Know? More than 140,000 people experience Science Central each year.

The Embassy Theatre

Originally known as the Emboyd Theatre, it opened in 1928 as a movie theater and vaudeville house. One of its signature features was a Page theatre pipe organ, but it was also notable for being attached to the 7-story, 250-room Indiana Hotel. When vaudeville was at its most popular, the Emboyd hosted comedians, magicians, acrobats, and musicians.

In 1952, the theatre and hotel were sold, and the name was changed to the Embassy Theatre. It operated as a movie theatre until 1971, when both the hotel and theatre closed. After extensive renovation, the theatre and hotel opened in 1995 for shows, community events, and private parties.

Best Time to Visit: The best time to visit the Embassy Theatre is when a show you want to attend is playing. Check the website for times and dates.

Pass/Permit/Fees: The fee to visit the Embassy Theatre depends on show and seat selection.

Closest City or Town: Fort Wayne

Physical Address: 125 W. Jefferson Boulevard, Fort Wayne, IN 46802

GPS Coordinates: 41.077664° N, 85.14023° W

Did You Know? The Walk of Recognition in the Embassy Theatre pays homage to Indiana natives who performed at the theatre throughout the years.

The History Center

The heritage of Fort Wayne comes alive at the History Center, located in the historic 1893 City Building. Numerous exhibits, photographs, and artifacts take visitors through Fort Wayne's history, from Chief Little Turtle of the Miami Native American tribe to General Anthony "Mad Anthony" Wayne, an American soldier who gave his name to Fort Wayne. The museum got its start in 1921, when the Allen County-Fort Wayne Historical Society was founded, and it now houses more than 32,000 artifacts related to the county's history. The City Building has been home to the society since 1980. Permanent exhibits include *Earliest Inhabitants*, *Miami History*, *An Emerging City*, and the *Old City Jail*.

Best Time to Visit: The History Center is open Monday through Friday from 10:00 a.m. to 5:00 p.m., Saturday from 12:00 p.m. to 5:00 p.m., and the first Sunday of each month from 12:00 p.m. to 5:00 p.m.

Pass/Permit/Fees: Admission is $6 for adults, $4 for children ages 3 to 17, $4 for seniors ages 65 and older, and free for children ages 2 and under.

Closest City or Town: Fort Wayne

Physical Address: 302 E. Berry Street, Fort Wayne, IN 46802

GPS Coordinates: 41.08062° N, 85.13608° W

Did You Know? The History Center also features a replica blacksmith shop and hosts the annual Gingerbread Festival.

Gary Aquatorium

The Gary Aquatorium opened in 1922 as the Lakefront Park Bathhouse. It was constructed to be a shower, changing room, and bathroom facility at Miller Beach in Marquette Park. The building is architecturally significant since it is an early example of pre-cast concrete modular construction. In fact, 90 percent of the structure was built with just six basic cast blocks, with the most basic being the T-block. Little maintenance was spent on the facility between 1922 and 1971, when it was boarded up and closed to the public. It was slated for demolition in 1991, but the Chanute Aquatorium Society stepped in to save it and in the process invented the word *aquatorium*, meaning "place to view the water." The facility is now a museum that honors Octave Chanute, who is considered the Father of Flight, and the Tuskegee Airmen who initiated the integration of the armed forces.

Best Time to Visit: The Gary Aquatorium is open 24 hours a day, and anyone can use it. However, special events should be scheduled ahead of time.

Pass/Permit/Fees: There is no fee to visit.

Closest City or Town: Gary

Physical Address: 6918 Oak Avenue, Gary, IN 46403

GPS Coordinates: 41.62052° N, 87.25722° W

Did You Know? There is also an open-air gallery and a secret garden at the aquatorium.

Indiana Birding Trail

The Indiana Birding Trail, located between the shores of Lake Michigan and the banks of the Ohio River, features over 400 bird species living in diverse habitats. The state is a migratory zone for birds flying between Argentina and the Arctic regions. Indiana's wetlands, prairies, and forests provide essential resources to all sorts of birds during their journey. At the northern end of the birding trail, you'll see a massive spring migratory gathering as birds conserve their energy and prepare to fly over Lake Michigan. Various birds come back to Indiana in the spring to mate and raise their young before heading further south.

Best Time to Visit: The best time to visit the Indiana Birding Trail is during the spring.

Pass/Permit/Fees: Parking fees will vary depending on where you access the trail.

Closest City or Town: Gary

Physical Address: The Indiana Birding Trail website offers an interactive map for detailed navigation of the many access points on this trail. One of the northernmost sites is the Hammond Lakefront Park and Bird Sanctuary, found at 701 Casino Center Drive, Hammond, IN 46320.

GPS Coordinates: 41.61969° N, 87.26461° W

Did You Know? Of the 400 bird species found along the Indiana Birding Trail, more than 360 have been identified along the shore of Lake Michigan in Indiana.

Marquette Park

Marquette Park has roots dating back to 1865 when settlers first began using the lakefront area for recreation and other activities. Near the turn of the century, Octave Chanute flew his gliders and biplanes on Miller Beach well before the Wright Brothers made their historic flight. At the north end of Lake Street, Carr's Bathhouse was a popular lakefront bathing facility, and beach cottages and a dance hall were nearby. The city of Gary decided to create a park area with access to the lake in 1912.

In the 1920s, work began to level the sand dune south of where the Gary Bathing Beach Pavilion would one day be. Originally called Lake Front Park, the recreation area was renamed Marquette Park after Pere Jacques Marquette, a French Jesuit missionary who established the first European settlement in Michigan.

Best Time to Visit: The best time to visit Marquette Park is in the summer, especially for water activities.

Pass/Permit/Fees: There is no fee to visit Marquette Park.

Closest City or Town: Gary

Physical Address: 1 N. Grand Boulevard, Gary, IN 46403

GPS Coordinates: 41.61969° N, 87.26461° W

Did You Know? In the 1930s, the city of Gary attempted to get funding to create a yacht club in the park. They were unable to secure federal aid, so they constructed a trapshooting range and clubhouse instead.

The Cathedral of the Holy Angels

Established in 1906, the Holy Angels Parish was the first
Catholic parish in Gary. Originally, the parish worshipped
in a tavern and then in a school–church combination. By
the 1940s, the parish had grown to the point where a new
church was necessary, and construction began on the
Cathedral of the Holy Angels in 1947. It was completed in
1950 in the Gothic Revival architectural style. Six years
later, the church was officially declared a cathedral. The
baptismal pool is constructed of travertine marble, and the
upper portion is made from black walnut. The marble altar
is surrounded by mosaic angels that represent the diversity
of the human race. Carved angels can also be found next to
the bishop's chair and on a cross behind the tabernacle.

Best Time to Visit: If you'd like to visit the cathedral
during Mass, visit on Sunday at 11:00 a.m. or Wednesday
at 5:30 p.m. Otherwise, the church is open Monday through
Friday from 8:30 a.m. to 4:30 p.m.

Pass/Permit/Fees: There is no fee to visit the cathedral.

Closest City or Town: Gary

Physical Address: 640 Tyler Street, Gary, IN 46402

GPS Coordinates: 41.59956° N, 87.34887° W

Did You Know? The cathedral's architecture has won
several awards, including the Excellence in Masonry
Award from the Illinois Indiana Masonry Council in 2002
and the 1999–2000 Visual Arts Awards for its altar.

18th Street Distillery

Opened in 2018, the 18th Street Distillery is the first award-winning artisan distillery to operate in Hammond since Prohibition. The distillery's process is noted for the time it takes to produce the highest-quality spirits with only the finest ingredients. This is true to the founder Drew Cox's philosophy that the distillery will not take shortcuts just to get their product on the shelves. The distillery is a spinoff of 18th Street Brewery, another popular attraction in town. Originally located in an old brick factory building, the distillery moved to a newer campus in 2020 that includes the 18th Street Brewery's production facility, restaurant, and taproom. The distillery expanded to include an outdoor entertainment area and an herb and botanical garden.

Best Time to Visit: The 18th Street Distillery is open Sunday from 11:00 a.m. to 8:00 p.m., Tuesday through Thursday from 4:00 p.m. to 10:00 p.m., Friday from 2:00 p.m. to 11:00 p.m., and Saturday from 11:00 a.m. to 11:00 p.m.

Pass/Permit/Fees: There is no cover charge.

Closest City or Town: Hammond

Physical Address: 5417 Oakley Avenue #1, Hammond, IN 46320

GPS Coordinates: 41.61573° N, 87.51716° W

Did You Know? Spirits that are produced in the distillery include vodka, rum, gin, and moonshine.

Aquatic Play Center

Located at Wolf Lake, the Aquatic Play Center is designed for children ages 12 and under who want to enjoy a state-of-the-art splash pad and playground. The center opened in 2016. Sessions are 1 hour and 45 minutes long and allow younger kids to enjoy water fun without the bigger kids taking over. The facility can be rented out for private parties. If you have kids who are older than 12, they can take part in the multitude of other activities in the park while an adult accompanies the younger kids to the Aquatic Play Center. The fountains, dump bucket, and fun play structures are great for cooling down on a hot day. The entire splash pad is fenced in to ensure safety.

Best Time to Visit: The Aquatic Play Center is open daily from 10:00 a.m. to 7:00 p.m., Memorial Day through Labor Day (weather permitting).

Pass/Permit/Fees: The fee to visit the Aquatic Play Center is $1 for Hammond and Whiting Residents ($2 on weekends), $2 for Indiana residents ($3 on weekends), and $3 for nonresidents ($4 on weekends).

Closest City or Town: Hammond

Physical Address: 2100 Calumet Avenue, Hammond, IN 46320

GPS Coordinates: 41.67520° N, 87.50900° W

Did You Know? Two parents or guardians are allowed into the Aquatic Play Center for free with one paid child admission.

Festival of the Lakes

This festival is 5 days of entertainment and activity on Wolf Lake, Lake Michigan, and Lake George. Usually held in July, the festival features popular live musical acts, amusement park rides, midway games, and food vendors. There are also numerous special events, including a polka party and a fishing derby. Musical acts have included Walker County, Jonny James, Twista, Nelly, Busta Rhymes, Limp Bizkit, REO Speedwagon, 3 Doors Down, and many more. Also on the annual schedule is a hot rod and custom car show, which includes door prizes, awards, and a DJ. Children, disabled guests, and seniors all have days that cater to their interests and needs. A charity walk and run called the Roadie 5K begins and ends at Wolf Lake Aquatic Play Center on the Saturday of the festival.

Best Time to Visit: The only time to visit the Festival of the Lakes is in July each year. Check the website for exact dates and event schedules.

Pass/Permit/Fees: There is a $30 fee per vehicle for parking.

Closest City or Town: Hammond

Physical Address: 2324 Calumet Avenue, Hammond, IN 46320

GPS Coordinates: 41.67546° N, 87.50930° W

Did You Know? The Festival of the Lakes has been an annual event since 1984.

Gibson Woods

A 179-acre nature preserve, Gibson Woods is known for its uncommon dune-and-swale ecosystem. The unlikely combination of high dunes and low wetlands provides a habitat for numerous rare and endangered plants. There are several hiking trails totaling 3.5 miles throughout the woods, and visitors are asked to stay on the marked paths to avoid damaging the fragile ecosystem. Within Gibson Woods, there is also an Environmental Awareness Center; a Wildlife Viewing Room; and a Bird, Insect, and Wildlife Hotspot. The Environmental Awareness Center opened in 1984 and offers exhibits such as live reptile and amphibian displays. When visiting the preserve, look for the dominant habitat of black oak savanna trees, along with bracken fern, big bluestem, tall coreopsis, mesic sand prairie, the rarer paper birch, Kalm's St. John's wort, and golden sedge.

Best Time to Visit: Visit during the spring for the wildflowers and the fall for the changing colors of the trees.

Pass/Permit/Fees: There is no fee to visit Gibson Woods.

Closest City or Town: Hammond

Physical Address: 6201 Parrish Avenue, Hammond, IN 46323

GPS Coordinates: 41.60074° N, 87.45135° W

Did You Know? The Gibson Woods Nature Preserve supports many wildlife species, including the plains pocket gopher, the Karner blue butterfly, Blanding's turtle, and the rare Franklin's ground squirrel.

Hammond Lakefront Park & Bird Sanctuary

Located on over a quarter mile of the lakefront on Lake Michigan, the Hammond Lakefront Park and Bird Sanctuary is a small space in the middle of an industrial area. It might seem like something you can pass up, but if you take the short, narrow trail at the right time of year, you'll see various neotropical birds that stop at the sanctuary during their migrations. Known as "The Migrant Trap," the sanctuary hosts large numbers of migrant passerines in spring and fall.

Other birds stop in the area throughout the year but in lesser numbers. There are even some species that winter on Lake Michigan, so you can still view waterfowl during the colder months as well. The pines located on the east side of the sanctuary are the best place to start looking for birds.

Best Time to Visit: The best times to visit are spring and fall during bird migrations.

Pass/Permit/Fees: There is no fee to visit.

Closest City or Town: Hammond

Physical Address: 701 Casino Center Drive, Hammond, IN 46320

GPS Coordinates: 41.70024° N, 87.51460° W

Did You Know? Only 16 acres in area, the Hammond Lakefront Park and Bird Sanctuary is a critical migration stopping point for more than 250 species of birds.

Towle Theater

Originally named the Towle Opera House when it opened in 1903, the Towle Theater was once also called the De Lux Theatre (1913), the DeLuxe Theatre (1926), and finally, the Towle Theater (2003). When it was built by Marcus M. Towle, the opera house was the most modern one in the country by far. It often featured the top theater productions in the region, which were considered equal to those in Chicago. Currently, the Towle Theater is a performing arts venue that is home to the Towle Performing Arts Company, a nonprofit organization that relies on support from the Hammond Urban Enterprise Association, the Hammond Port Authority, the City of Hammond, and Mayor Thomas M. McDermott, along with patron donations.

Best Time to Visit: The best time to visit the Towle Theater is when you want to see a performance. Check the website for dates and times.

Pass/Permit/Fees: Ticket costs vary from show to show.

Closest City or Town: Hammond

Physical Address: 5205 Hohman Avenue, Hammond, IN 46320

GPS Coordinates: 41.61949° N, 87.52096° W

Did You Know? During the building's history, the space now occupied by the theater was at times a department store (1931), a grocery store (1935), and various specialty stores (1939–1960s).

Wolf Lake Park and Pavilion

The Pavilion at Wolf Lake Park is the premier outdoor venue for movies, concerts, and festivals for Northwest Indiana. Locally known as "The PAV," the design was inspired by the 1895 amusement resort concept imagined by Frank Lloyd Wright. The main stage is 2,600 square feet in area, and 86,000 square feet is available for seating. Boating, fishing, windsurfing, and kayaking are popular activities on the lake, and the Wolf Lake Aquatic Play Center provides hours of entertainment for young swimmers. Hiking is also available on the pedestrian trail that takes visitors to the Hammond Marina and other park amenities. The park and pavilion host the annual Festival of the Lakes, which takes place in July and features food, rides, and musical performances.

Best Time to Visit: The best time to visit Wolf Lake Park and Pavilion is in the summer for water activities and musical performances.

Pass/Permit/Fees: There is no charge to visit Wolf Lake Park and Pavilion, but there may be a fee for festivals, concerts, or water-equipment rentals.

Closest City or Town: Hammond

Physical Address: 2324 Calumet Avenue, Hammond, IN 46320

GPS Coordinates: 42.58035° N, 87.56558° W

Did You Know? Each year, the Wolf Lake Park and Pavilion hosts the Fourth of July naturalization ceremony.

Bad Axe Throwing

At Bad Axe Throwing, you can learn how to throw an axe at a target in the tradition of the Canadians, who have participated in this activity in their own backyards for decades. The world's biggest axe-throwing club was founded by Mario Zelaya in 2014. Since then, thousands of customers have taken part in the sport. There are more than 40 locations in North America, and the Indianapolis branch has been rated the go-to destination. In addition to axe throwing, a large selection of brand-name and craft beers are available for patrons who are 21 years of age or older. Lanes are meant for four or more people, but limited walk-in hours are available throughout the week for groups with fewer than four people.

Best Time to Visit: Bad Axe Throwing is open Monday from 6:00 p.m. to 9:00 p.m., Tuesday from 4:30 p.m. to 10:00 p.m., Wednesday from 5:30 p.m. to 10:00 p.m., Thursday from 2:00 p.m. to 10:00 p.m., and Friday from 12:00 p.m. to 11:00 p.m.

Pass/Permit/Fees: The fee to visit Bad Axe Throwing is $26.98 per person. Group rates are also available.

Closest City or Town: Indianapolis

Physical Address: 235 S. Meridian Street #211, Indianapolis, IN 46225

GPS Coordinates: 39.76402° N, 86.15815° W

Did You Know? The practice of axe throwing dates all the way back to 400–500 CE.

Children's Museum of Indianapolis

Founded in 1925, the Children's Museum of Indianapolis began in the Carriage House of the Propylaeum and moved to the Shelter House in Garfield Park a year later. In 1927, it moved again to its founder's home, the Mary Stewart Carey House. Finally, it found a permanent home in a limestone mansion known as the Parry House at 30th and Meridian streets in 1946.

In 1976, a new 5-story dedicated museum structure was constructed at the site of the Parry House, making it the largest children's museum in the world. Along with the galleries, the new space included the Ruth Allison Lilly Theater. The museum hosts special events for all ages. Check the museum's website for current functions.

Best Time to Visit: The museum is open daily from 10:00 a.m. to 5:00 p.m. in the spring and summer. In the fall and winter, it's open Tuesday through Sunday from 10:00 a.m. to 5:00 p.m.

Pass/Permit/Fees: The fee to visit the Children's Museum of Indianapolis varies by day. See the website for rates.

Closest City or Town: Indianapolis

Physical Address: 3000 N. Meridian Street, Indianapolis, IN 46208

GPS Coordinates: 39.81114° N, 86.15806° W

Did You Know? First Lady Eleanor Roosevelt visited a WPA workers' doll collection at the museum in 1937.

Crown Hill Cemetery

Crown Hill Cemetery is the third-largest non-government cemetery in the country. While it is primarily a cemetery, there are many other activities that visitors find interesting. They enjoy the blooming flowers in the spring, the incredible fall foliage in the autumn, and even the frosty landscape in the winter.

You can take a cemetery tour that's led by a knowledgeable guide who will tell you amazing stories about the architecture, tombstones, trees, and history of the cemetery. Nearly all tours will take you to the top of the crown, where you'll get a panoramic view of the Indianapolis skyline from the highest point in Marion County.

Best Time to Visit: Spring and fall are the best times to visit to see the flowers in bloom or the changing colors of the trees.

Pass/Permit/Fees: There is no fee to visit Crown Hill Cemetery, but tours start at $10 for adults and $5 for children ages 5 to 17.

Closest City or Town: Indianapolis

Physical Address: 700 38th Street, Indianapolis, IN 46208

GPS Coordinates: 39.82636° N, 86.17221° W

Did You Know? Events such as Memorial Day and the Spirit of Freedom Civil War Program feature re-enactments of significant pivot points in history.

Eagle Creek Park

Eagle Creek Park is the former site of J. K. Lilly Jr.'s Eagle Crest Estate, which included a lodge, swimming pool, watchman's cabin, and library (currently the Ornithology Center). Lilly also purchased three farms nearby and named them Eagle Valley Farms. He acquired more land east of Eagle Creek, reforested it, and named it Eagle Crest Forest Reserve. Eventually, Lilly donated all of his estate, the farms, and the forest to Purdue University before a flood in 1957 led to the proposal to dam Eagle Creek and build a reservoir. The City of Indianapolis bought 2,286 acres from Purdue University to create the dam and resulting park. Over time, the Eagle Creek Park Nature Center (now the Ornithology Center), the Fitness Trail, the Scott Starling Nature Sanctuary, and the Earth Discovery Center were added to the park.

Best Time to Visit: The best time to visit Eagle Creek Park is in the spring, summer, or fall.

Pass/Permit/Fees: There is a daily use fee of $5 for in-state vehicles, $6 for out-of-state vehicles, and $1.50 for walk-in visitors.

Closest City or Town: Indianapolis

Physical Address: 7840 W. 56th Street, Indianapolis, IN 46254

GPS Coordinates: 39.87409° N, 86.29620° W

Did You Know? Eagle Creek is the fourth-largest municipal park in the U.S.

74

Eiteljorg Museum of American Indian and Western Art

Built in 1989, the Eiteljorg Museum of American Indian and Western Art was founded to help the community appreciate and understand the art, cultures, and history of the American West and North American Indigenous peoples. Visitors can immerse themselves in the diversity of these cultures and listen to their incredible stories. The building was designed to reflect the Western and Native American stories that are told inside. The 118,000-square-foot building is set inside a large, round base inspired by the Native Pueblo communities, who often use circular symbols in their art. The stone, honey-colored Minnesota dolomite gives the impression of a traditional Southwestern Pueblo.

Best Time to Visit: The museum is open Monday through Saturday from 10:00 a.m. to 5:00 p.m. and Sunday from 12:00 p.m. to 5:00 p.m.

Pass/Permit/Fees: Admission is $15 for adults, $8 for children, and $12 for seniors.

Closest City or Town: Indianapolis

Physical Address: 500 W. Washington Street, Indianapolis, IN 46204

GPS Coordinates: 39.76943° N, 86.16792° W

Did You Know? The Eiteljorg Museum is one of only two museums east of the Mississippi that feature both the American West and Native Americans.

Fort Harrison State Park

This 1,700-acre park features numerous amenities, including trails, picnic sites, fishing spots, and two national historic districts. Once the site of Camp Glen, a citizen's military training camp, Fort Harrison State Park also boasts one of the biggest sledding hills in the region. In the spring, visitors enjoy the blooming woodland wildflowers, and in the summer, they can get their thrills by taking a canoe trip down Fall Creek. Fall is also a great time to visit to see the colorful foliage in all its autumn glory. The park is home to the Museum of 20th Century Warfare, which has displays about the history and lives of the U.S. soldiers who once lived at Fort Harrison. This park is truly an oasis of nature in the middle of the big city.

Best Time to Visit: The park offers activities all year long, which makes it perfect to visit anytime.

Pass/Permit/Fees: There is a $7 daily fee for in-state vehicles and a $9 daily fee for out-of-state vehicles. Walk-ins are $2 per person.

Closest City or Town: Indianapolis

Physical Address: 6000 N. Post Road, Indianapolis, IN 46216

GPS Coordinates: 39.86869° N, 86.02025° W

Did You Know? Fort Harrison State Park is named for Indianapolis native U.S. President Benjamin Harrison. The military facility opened in 1902 and closed for those purposes in the 1990s.

Goose the Market

This full-service butcher shop and specialty food market has a rotating menu of soups, sandwiches, craft beer, and wine. Its cases are stocked with cheeses; house-made sausages; cured meats; and local steaks, chops, and poultry. Goose the Market has been a staple in Indianapolis for more than a decade and has been profiled by national food publications like *Bon Appetit*, *The New York Times*, and *Food & Wine*, among others. Goose's wine cellar, Enoteca, is open to patrons ages 21 and older to enjoy beer and wine by the glass along with cheese, cured-meat tasting flights, and small tasting plates. Locally referred to as "The Goose," this market was built around a passion for excellent food, the people who spend their lives making it, and the people who can't wait to taste it.

Best Time to Visit: The market is open Monday through Friday from 10:00 a.m. to 8:00 a.m. and Saturday and Sunday from 10:00 a.m. to 6:00 p.m.

Pass/Permit/Fees: There is no fee to visit Goose the Market, but be prepared to spend some money on awesome food and beverages.

Closest City or Town: Indianapolis

Physical Address: 2503 N. Delaware Street, Indianapolis, IN 46205

GPS Coordinates: 39.80383° N, 86.15281° W

Did You Know? Many culinary events and lessons regularly take place at Goose the Market.

Holliday Park

Located 6 miles north of downtown Indianapolis, this is one of the city's oldest parks. It became a park in 1916 during the centennial celebration of Indiana's statehood, when John and Evaline Holliday donated their estate to the city. Their intention was for the open space to become a recreation area, which was fulfilled with the creation of Holliday Park.

At 96 acres, there is plenty of space for visitors to enjoy the nature center, playgrounds, hiking trails, and Holliday Park Ruins. It's a great way for people to get into nature without leaving the city. The Ruins arrived in the 1950s when the St. Paul Building in New York City was demolished to make room for a skyscraper. A contest was held to find a new home for that building's façade and three associated Indiana-limestone statues. Indianapolis came out on top.

Best Time to Visit: Visit during the spring or fall for milder weather, blooming flowers, and colorful foliage.

Pass/Permit/Fees: There is no fee to visit Holliday Park.

Closest City or Town: Indianapolis

Physical Address: 6363 Spring Mill Road, Indianapolis, IN 46260

GPS Coordinates: 39.87221° N, 86.16113° W

Did You Know? The Ruins were inaccessible to the public for more than two decades before being revitalized and updated as part of a $3.2-million project in 2016.

Indiana Medical History Museum

The Indiana Medical History Museum is housed in the buildings of the former Central State Hospital. The main portion of the museum is in the Old Pathology Building, which is the oldest pathology facility in the country still in existence. The Pathological Department was established in 1896 to further medical education and research on the biological causes of mental disease. It operated until the 1960s and became a museum in 1969. It was preserved just as it was left on the last day it was open. Tours are available of the teaching amphitheater, bacteriology laboratories, chemistry clinic, library, records room, reception room, and autopsy room. You can also visit the anatomical museum, which includes preserved specimens arranged by pathology.

Best Time to Visit: The museum is open for tours Wednesday through Saturday by appointment only.

Pass/Permit/Fees: Admission is $10 for adults, $5 for children under age 18, $7 for students with ID, and $9 for seniors ages 65 and older.

Closest City or Town: Indianapolis

Physical Address: 3270 Kirkbride Way, Indianapolis, IN 46222

GPS Coordinates: 39.77087° N, 86.21342° W

Did You Know? Central State Hospital was originally named the Indiana Hospital for the Insane, which opened in 1848 to treat people with various mental conditions.

Indiana State Capitol

The original capital of Indiana was Corydon, but it was relocated to Indianapolis in 1825 and plans for the capitol building were drawn up in 1867. The decision to move the capital from Corydon to Indianapolis resulted from the influx of northern settlers who required a more centrally located seat of government. It was 1888 before the capitol building was completed. Built from Indiana white oak and limestone, the capitol building has stood the test of time, as it is still the center of civic life in the state.

It houses all executive offices, the Indiana House of Representatives, the Indiana State Senate, and the Indiana State Supreme Court. The first statehouse building, which was constructed in 1835, no longer stands because it was replaced with the current structure.

Best Time to Visit: The Indiana State Capitol is open for tours Monday through Friday from 9:00 a.m. to 3:00 p.m. and Saturday from 10:00 a.m. to 1:00 p.m.

Pass/Permit/Fees: There is no fee to visit the capitol.

Closest City or Town: Indianapolis

Physical Address: 200 W. Washington Street, Indianapolis, IN 46204

GPS Coordinates: 39.76947° N, 86.16264° W

Did You Know? The Indiana State Capitol building underwent an extensive renovation 100 years after its completion.

Indiana State Museum

The Indiana State Museum is located in White River State Park in Indianapolis. Its interactive exhibits and engaging experiences tell the stories of the people and events that helped create the state as it is today. The building itself is an architectural gem built entirely from Indiana sandstone, limestone, brick, steel, and glass. Each of the 92 icons integrated into the structure's exterior walls represents one of Indiana's counties.

The 3-story museum features both permanent and temporary exhibits that convey Indiana's culture and history. The museum's roots date back to 1869 when the Indiana General Assembly passed a law to collect and preserve the natural history of the state.

Best Time to Visit: The museum is open Wednesday through Sunday from 10:00 a.m. to 5:00 p.m.

Pass/Permit/Fees: Admission is $17 for adults, $12 for children ages 3 to 17, $16 for seniors ages 60 and older, and free for children under the age of 3.

Closest City or Town: Indianapolis, Indiana

Physical Address: 650 W Washington St, Indianapolis, IN 46204

GPS Coordinates: 39.76918° N, 86.16972° W

Did You Know? The Indiana State Museum moved out of its home in old city hall in 2001 and into its new quarters, built around an existing IMAX Theater, in 2002.

Indianapolis Art Center

The Indianapolis Art Center originated as the Indianapolis Art Students League, which was designed in 1934 to serve artists during the Great Depression. Since its humble beginnings, the Art Center has evolved to showcasing art in exhibits at six art galleries, offering hundreds of art classes, establishing an outreach program to bring art to underserved communities, and hosting the annual OneAmerica Broad Ripple Art Fair.

It moved to its current location on the banks of the White River in 1976, and the Art Center added a sculpture garden called ARTSPARK in 2005. This 9.5-acre garden was designed by an Indiana native, architect Michael Graves.

Best Time to Visit: The museum is open Monday through Friday from 9:00 a.m. to 10:00 p.m., Saturday from 9:00 a.m. to 6:00 p.m., and Sunday from 12:00 p.m. to 6:00 p.m.

Pass/Permit/Fees: There is no fee to visit the Indianapolis Art Center, but donations are appreciated.

Closest City or Town: Indianapolis

Physical Address: 820 E. 67th Street, Indianapolis, IN 46220

GPS Coordinates: 39.87854° N, 86.14392° W

Did You Know? The interactive sculptures throughout the garden are meant to evoke all five senses. They include a variety of colors, patterns, textures, sounds, and even smells.

Indianapolis City Market

This historic public marketplace was founded in 1821 and opened in its current location in 1886. The market is housed in a one-story brick building that's trimmed with Indiana limestone. Its front gable center section is flanked by two square towers. It was originally a farmers market but has expanded to include more than 30 artisan vendors offering fresh local produce, crafts, and other unique items. It's the ideal place to visit if you want to dine out, grab some fresh ingredients to dine in, or find a special gift. The Indianapolis City Market is one of the longest-running and largest markets in the state. In addition to food and gifts, you can even get a haircut at the market's barbershop or pick out some fresh flowers from the local florist, the Flower Boys.

Best Time to Visit: The Indianapolis City Market is open Monday and Tuesday from 7:00 a.m. to 4:00 p.m., Wednesday through Friday from 7:00 a.m. to 9:00 p.m., and on Saturday from 8:00 a.m. to 6:00 p.m.

Pass/Permit/Fees: There is no fee to visit the market, but bring some money to spend on local food and crafts.

Closest City or Town: Indianapolis

Physical Address: 222 E. Market Street, Indianapolis, IN 46204

GPS Coordinates: 39.76937° N, 86.15356° W

Did You Know? The Indianapolis City Market was placed on the National Register of Historic Places in 1974.

Indianapolis Cultural Trail

This Indianapolis Culture Trail takes visitors through six cultural districts that were designated in 1999: Fountain Square, Indiana Avenue, Massachusetts Avenue, the Canal & White River State Park, Broad Ripple, and the Wholesale District. Plans were laid to build an 8-mile-long, world-class urban pedestrian and bike trail winding through downtown Indianapolis.

The trail officially opened in 2013, having been under construction since April 2007. Currently, there are plans to expand the trail to Capitol Avenue from South Street and to 10th Street from Indiana Avenue. This expansion will bring in additional culturally and historically significant neighborhoods and destinations that should be considered parts of downtown Indianapolis.

Best Time to Visit: The best time to visit the trail is during the spring or fall when the weather is cooler.

Pass/Permit/Fees: There is no fee.

Closest City or Town: Indianapolis

Physical Address: 132 W. Walnut Street, Indianapolis, IN 46204

GPS Coordinates: 39.77782° N, 86.16135° W

Did You Know? Along the Indianapolis Cultural Trail, $4 million of public art commissioned by the Curatorial Advisory Committee is on display. Look for *Ann Dancing*, *Looking Through Windows*, *Poet's Place*, and more.

Indianapolis Motor Speedway Museum

Established in 1956, the Indianapolis Motor Speedway Museum is conveniently located inside the famous 2.5-mile Indianapolis Motor Speedway track. Its 37,500 square feet of exhibit space features race cars, photographs, trophies, memorabilia, fine art, and racing records to tell the story of automobile racing both nationally and internationally. More than 140,000 people visit the museum every year to view the museum's collection of IndyCar, NASCAR, USAC Sprints, Formula One, Midgets, motorcycle racing, and drag-racing artifacts. There are also several passenger automobiles on display, most of which were manufactured in Indiana by enterprises that were intimately connected to racing.

Best Time to Visit: Between March and October, the museum is open daily from 9:00 a.m. to 5:00 p.m. Between November and February, it's open daily from 10:00 a.m. to 4:00 p.m.

Pass/Permit/Fees: Admission is $15 for adults, $8 for children ages 6 to 15, $14 for seniors ages 62 and older, and free for children ages 5 and under.

Closest City or Town: Indianapolis

Physical Address: 4750 W. 16th Street, Indianapolis, IN 46222

GPS Coordinates: 39.79048° N, 86.23361° W

Did You Know? The museum has been named one of *USA Today*'s top three sports attractions in the nation.

Indianapolis Museum of Art

The Indianapolis Museum of Art on the Newfields campus is one of the largest and oldest art museums in the country. Its permanent collection features more than 50,000 works of art, including one of the country's largest collections of Asian Art and the Eiteljorg Suite of African and Oceanic Art. Outside the museum, visitors can tour the historic Oldfields Estate, the 1920s-inspired gardens, the Virginia B. Fairbanks Art & Nature Park, and the *Five Brushstrokes* sculpture. There are over 152 acres of art in the museum and on the grounds representing an immense range of eras and cultures. There is plenty to explore and something for every artistic taste.

Best Time to Visit: The museum is open Sunday, Tuesday, and Wednesday from 11:00 a.m. to 5:00 p.m. and Thursday through Saturday from 11:00 a.m. to 8:00 p.m.

Pass/Permit/Fees: Admission is $18 for adults, $10 for children ages 6 to 17, and free for children ages 5 and under.

Closest City or Town: Indianapolis

Physical Address: 4000 N. Michigan Road, Indianapolis, IN 46208

GPS Coordinates: 39.82659° N, 86.18596° W

Did You Know? A special Meet Me tour is offered at the museum for guests with early-stage Alzheimer's to enjoy a facilitated conversation about the art.

Indianapolis Zoo

Home to over 3,800 animals from approximately 320 species and subspecies, the Indianapolis Zoo opened in1964. The concept was initially broached in 1944 by Lowell B. Nussbaum, a newspaperman who wrote about the city's need for a zoo. His idea inspired Indianapolis residents to support the idea, but it took 20 years for the goal to be realized. It originally opened in George Washington Park and drew 270,000 visitors its first year. By 1984, attendance had doubled, and it was clear that a larger facility was necessary. The old location closed in 1987, and the new facility in White River State Park opened as both a zoo and an aquarium.

Best Time to Visit: The Indianapolis Zoo is open Monday through Thursday from 9:00 a.m. to 5:00 p.m. and Friday through Sunday from 9:00 a.m. to 7:00 p.m.

Pass/Permit/Fees: Admission is $29.75 for adults, $25.75 for children ages 2 to 12, and $27.75 for seniors ages 62 and older. Zoo parking is $8 per vehicle.

Closest City or Town: Indianapolis

Physical Address: 1200 W. Washington Street, Indianapolis, IN 46222

GPS Coordinates: 39.76668° N, 86.18113° W

Did You Know? With the inclusion of White River Gardens in 2006, the Indianapolis Zoo is the first facility to be triple accredited as a zoo, aquarium, and botanical garden.

Kurt Vonnegut Museum and Library

This museum is a tribute to the late author, artist, and Indianapolis native Kurt Vonnegut Jr. Established in 2011 and moved to a new building in 2019, the museum is a combination library, art gallery, reading room, and educational facility. One of its main goals is to support visual arts and language education through outreach programs, on-site activities, and collaboration with other local arts organizations. Among the exhibits are artifacts from Vonnegut's life, including his Smith-Corona Coronamatic 2200 typewriter, an unopened letter that his father sent him during World War II, rejection letters from magazines, and a full replica of his writing studio. In the art gallery, you'll discover works from national and local artists.

Best Time to Visit: The museum and library are open Monday, Friday, and Saturday from 10:00 a.m. to 7:00 p.m. and Sunday from 10:00 a.m. to 5:30 p.m.

Pass/Permit/Fees: Admission is $12 for adults, $7 for students, and $11 for seniors ages 65 and older.

Closest City or Town: Indianapolis

Physical Address: 543 Indiana Avenue, Indianapolis, IN 46202

GPS Coordinates: 39.77597° N, 86.16640° W

Did You Know? Special events, such as writing workshops and book groups, are available to veterans in honor of Kurt Vonnegut's military service.

Lilly House and Gardens

Located on the Newfields art complex, the Lilly House was originally built in 1913 for Hugh McKennan Landon, and it's the main attraction on the Oldfields Estate. J. K. Lilly Jr., an Indianapolis businessman, philanthropist, and art collector, purchased the house in 1932 and lived in it until he passed away in 1965. The house is a perfect example of an early 20th-century country estate, and the first floor has been carefully restored to resemble its appearance in the 1930s. The upper floor of the house offers a space for community events and public programs. If possible, check out the incredible panoramic view of the Oldfields gardens and estate by climbing the stairs to the second level.

Best Time to Visit: The Lilly House and Gardens are open Sunday, Tuesday, and Wednesday from 11:00 a.m. to 5:00 p.m. and Thursday through Saturday from 11:00 a.m. to 8:00 p.m.

Pass/Permit/Fees: Admission is $18 for adults and $10 for children ages 6 to 17.

Closest City or Town: Indianapolis

Physical Address: 4000 N. Michigan Road, Indianapolis, IN 46208

GPS Coordinates: 39.82903° N, 86.18522° W

Did You Know? Be sure to visit the Lilly House garage to see a car from the early 1900s that's on loan from the Indianapolis Motor Speedway Museum.

Lockerbie Square Historic District

As the oldest remaining residential neighborhood in the downtown area of Indianapolis, the Lockerbie Square Historic District showcases homes built by immigrants between 1821 and the late 19th century. There are numerous examples of the popular cottages and well-preserved high-style brick houses of the era. The oldest homes in the district can be found in the original Mile Square. In Indianapolis during this time, wealthy families and middle-class workers lived side by side, so you'll see the 1863 Johan Despa House just down the street from the statelier Charles Holstein House, where James Whitcomb Riley, the most famous Lockerbie Square resident, once rented a room from the Holsteins. The construction boom in Lockerbie Square slowed by 1910, and industry began to move into the area in the 1920s.

Best Time to Visit: Visit the district during the spring or fall when the weather is milder.

Pass/Permit/Fees: There is no fee to visit Lockerbie Square Historic District.

Closest City or Town: Indianapolis

Physical Address: 342–332 N. Park Avenue, Indianapolis, IN 46202

GPS Coordinates: 39.77284° N, 86.14728° N

Did You Know? During the mid-1800s, Lockerbie Square was known as Germantown because of the large number of German immigrants who moved into the neighborhood.

Lucas Oil Stadium

Home of the National Football League's Indianapolis Colts, Lucas Oil Stadium officially opened in fall 2008. The $720 million facility was financed through funds raised by the city of Indianapolis, the state of Indiana, and the Indianapolis Colts. Lucas Oil Products purchased the stadium's naming rights for $122 million over a 20-year term. With seating for approximately 67,000 fans for football and more than 70,000 fans for basketball, conventions, and concerts, Lucas Oil Stadium is one of the premier event venues in the state. The east sideline, west sideline, and north end zone are retractable, and the north end-zone seating can be removed to make even more space available for larger productions. The field is covered with artificial turf that weighs more than 820,000 pounds.

Best Time to Visit: The best time to visit Lucas Oil Stadium is during football season in the fall and winter.

Pass/Permit/Fees: The fee to visit Lucas Oil Stadium depends on event and seat selection.

Closest City or Town: Indianapolis

Physical Address: 500 S. Capitol Avenue, Indianapolis, IN 46225

GPS Coordinates: 39.76083° N, 86.16402° W

Did You Know? The two-panel retractable roof weighs 5 million pounds. It's the first of its kind and can be opened in about 11 minutes.

Market Street Catacombs

Beneath the Indianapolis City Market is an unusual attraction that many visitors pass by without ever knowing it's there. The Market Street Catacombs are a system of tunnels and Roman-style brick arches below Whistler Plaza. The catacombs are the remnants of Tomlinson Hall, an 1886 public building that once seated 3,500 people for various community events. City Market, which was constructed that same year, remains a vibrant part of downtown Indianapolis, but Tomlinson Hall burned to the ground in 1958, leaving only the building's iconic arch and its basement as reminders of its existence. While there are no bones or crypts in these catacombs, they are still fascinating to explore as part of a guided tour.

Best Time to Visit: Tours are only available on Saturday from May through October. They run every 15 minutes beginning at 10:00 a.m. Check the website for dates.

Pass/Permit/Fees: The fee to tour the catacombs is $12 for adults and $6 for children ages 6 to 11.

Closest City or Town: Indianapolis

Physical Address: 222 E. Market Street, Indianapolis, IN 46204

GPS Coordinates: 39.76933° N, 86.15359° W

Did You Know? When Indianapolis firefighters battled the blaze at Tomlinson Hall in 1958, Market Street was transformed into an icy lake from the volume of water used in the attempt to save the building.

Monument Circle

Monument Circle is the area of downtown Indianapolis that surrounds the Soldiers and Sailors Monument, which symbolizes both the city and state. The monument, which is constructed from limestone, was designed by Bruno Schmitz and built between 1887 and 1902. The sculpture is three different works of art: one by Rudolf Schwartz, who is responsible for the figures on the sides of the sculpture; one by George Brewster, who created *Victory*, the figure that tops the monument; and two astragals by Nicolaus Geiger. Visitors can access an observation level of this monument by climbing 330 steps or taking an elevator to step 290 and climbing 40 steps. Monument Circle is the site for numerous city-wide events throughout the year.

Best Time to Visit: While the monument can be visited any time of the year, the best time to visit Monument Circle is during an event that you want to attend. Check the website for dates and times.

Pass/Permit/Fees: There is no fee to visit Monument Circle, but various events may have separate entrance fees.

Closest City or Town: Indianapolis

Physical Address: Monument Circle, Indianapolis, IN 46204

GPS Coordinates: 39.76990° N, 86.15865° W

Did You Know? The monument is 284 feet tall and 342 feet in diameter.

Museum of Psychphonics

This eclectic museum tells the lesser-known stories of the state's history and its link to African American music. It also has other general themes of Afrofuturism and music of the spheres. The entrance to the museum, which resembles a small record store, hides the magnificence you'll encounter when you pass behind a heavy red curtain to the exhibits. You'll find antique musical instruments and memorabilia such as the ashtray from the Burger King where someone supposedly saw Elvis after he died. There are even dirt samples from places where UFOs have been seen and where famous musicians performed their last concerts. The featured object of the museum is the Parliament Funkadelic Baby Mothership that flew over about 300 audiences during the ParliaMent Funkadelic's road show. The baby mothership would land on stage and George Clinton would emerge from a larger mothership.

Best Time to Visit: The museum is only open on the first Friday of each month from 6:00 p.m. to 9:00 p.m.

Pass/Permit/Fees: There is no fee to visit the Museum of Psychphonics.

Closest City or Town: Indianapolis

Physical Address: 1043 Virginia Avenue, Indianapolis, IN 46203

GPS Coordinates: 39.75362° N, 86.14147° W

Did You Know? The baby mothership was the inspiration for the Museum of Psychphonics.

Rhythm! Discovery Center

Established in 2009, Rhythm! Discovery Center is the only interactive drum and percussion museum in the world. Visitors will discover hands-on exhibits that display a large collection of percussion instruments and historic musical artifacts. You'll find instruments that once belonged to leading percussionists and learn about playing techniques that will enhance your appreciation of percussion music.

Depending on when you visit, you may also be able to attend live musical performances. The facility boasts 13,500 square feet of exhibition space that is packed with instruments, many of which are meant for visitors to play.

Best Time to Visit: Rhythm! Discovery Center is open Sunday from 12:00 p.m. to 5:00 p.m. and Monday, Friday, and Saturday from 10:00 a.m. to 5:00 p.m.

Pass/Permit/Fees: Admission is $12 for adults, $6 for children ages 6 to 16, $9 for students, $8 for seniors, and free for children ages 5 and under.

Closest City or Town: Indianapolis

Physical Address: 110 W. Washington Street A, Indianapolis, IN 46204

GPS Coordinates: 39.76800° N, 86.16016° W

Did You Know? Donated percussion instruments at Rhythm! Discovery Center include those from Roy Knapp, Carroll Bratman, Haskell Harr, Shelly Manne, and many more.

Victory Field

Home of the Indianapolis Indians, a triple-A minor league affiliate of the Pittsburgh Pirates, Victory Field opened in 1996 with a game between the Indians and the Oklahoma City 89ers. Victory Field replaced Bush Stadium, which had been the team's home for 25 years. Although Victory Field was originally designed to seat 13,300 fans, it set a record of 16,168 in attendance at a game between the Indians and the Columbus Clippers on July 22, 2000. It has also played host to the 2001 Triple-A All-Star Game and annually hosts the Indiana Hoosiers baseball team for one game each year. In addition, the Indiana High School Athletic Association uses Victory Field for its state final baseball games for high school teams. The name Victory Field commemorates the U.S. victory in World War II.

Best Time to Visit: The best time to visit is during baseball season, which runs from spring until early fall.

Pass/Permit/Fees: The fee to visit Victory Field depends on game and seat selection.

Closest City or Town: Indianapolis

Physical Address: 501 W. Maryland Street, Indianapolis, IN 46225

GPS Coordinates: 39.76530° N, 86.16880° W

Did You Know? Victory Field has been named the "Best Minor League Ballpark in America" by *Sports Illustrated* and *Baseball America*. Most recently, it was the sixth-ranked stadium by *Baseball America* in 2015.

White Rabbit Cabaret

You never know exactly what you're going to see on stage at the White Rabbit Cabaret. It could be national or local musical acts, burlesque or cabaret entertainment, stand-up or improv comedy, or movie screenings. There's always something fun to experience at this facility in downtown Indianapolis. You have to be age 21 or over to enter the club, and you're sure to be enthralled with any show. Among the highly recommended shows are the Burlesque Bingo Bango Show, Lloyd & Harvey's Wowie Zowie Show, Burlesque Ballyhoo, and Hasenpfeffer. Other events include slam poetry nights, storytelling, dance parties, and vaudeville-style variety shows. Among the headliners are Bobcat Goldthwait, Adam Burke, Samia, John Craigie, Michael Malone, Clark Beckham, and Garcia Peoples.

Best Time to Visit: Performances are held year round at the White Rabbit Cabaret on Wednesday, Thursday, and Friday evenings.

Pass/Permit/Fees: The fee to visit the White Rabbit Cabaret depends on the show selected. Check the website for ticket prices.

Closest City or Town: Indianapolis

Physical Address: 1015 Olive Street, Indianapolis, IN 46203

GPS Coordinates: 39.75326° N, 86.13924° W

Did You Know? Seating is first-come, first-served, so get to the club early for seats!

White River State Park

The 250-acre White River State Park is a world-class destination that features hiking trails, greenspaces, waterways, educational activities, and cultural attractions. Located in downtown Indianapolis, White River State Park is a natural oasis in the middle of a bustling city. It was established in 1979 but didn't open until 1988. Other attractions added to the park over the years include the Eiteljorg Museum of American Indians & Western Art, Victory Field, an IMAX Theater, the NCAA Hall of Champions Museum, the Indiana State Museum, and the Lawn at White River State Park. Numerous events are held in the park, including Circle the City, Yappy Hour, and dozens of musical concerts.

Best Time to Visit: You can visit for a specific attraction or come any time to see what's available. It's best to visit in the spring or fall if you're here for the natural features in the park.

Pass/Permit/Fees: There is no fee to visit White River State Park, but there may be fees for events. Each attraction also has its own fees, so see individual websites for pricing.

Closest City or Town: Indianapolis

Physical Address: 801 W. Washington Street, Indianapolis, IN 46204

GPS Coordinates: 39.76641° N, 86.17066° W

Did You Know? The first attraction at White River State Park was the Indianapolis Zoo.

Salamonie River State Forest

In the 1930s, most of the topsoil in Indiana forests had been eroded away, and it was critical for the state to figure out how to reclaim the land and repopulate the forests. Salamonie River State Forest was established as a demonstration riverside forest to show how it could be done. A 200-member Civilian Conservation Corps (CCC) camp was created to plan the forest, open a stone quarry, and develop recreation facilities. This resulted in the reforestation of several hundred acres and the construction of numerous recreation facilities to bring visitors to the area. One such facility is Hominy Ridge Lake, a 4-acre body of water that offers fishing, boating, and swimming opportunities. Other activities popular in the forest include camping, hiking, and hunting for whitetail deer, turkey, fox, raccoon, and squirrel. Fishermen can expect to catch their fill of catfish, bluegill, and largemouth bass.

Best Time to Visit: Visit the forest during the summer.

Pass/Permit/Fees: There is no fee to visit the forest.

Closest City or Town: Lagro

Physical Address: 5124 County Road 100 S, Lagro, IN 46941

GPS Coordinates: 40.80988° N, 85.69066° W

Did You Know? Salamonie, the name for the forest, comes from the Native American word *O-sah-mo-nee*, meaning "yellow paint." Native American tribes made yellow paint from the bloodroot plant that grows in the forest.

Lincoln Boyhood National Memorial

In 1816, when Abraham Lincoln was 5 years old, he and his family moved to Indiana from his birthplace in Kentucky. They resided in the state until 1830 when Lincoln was 21, so Indiana was where the future president grew from a boy into a man. The Lincoln Boyhood National Memorial pays tribute to Lincoln's formative years, where he developed his honesty, compassion, respect for hard work, belief in education, and moral convictions that would one day guide him through one of the most tumultuous times in the nation's history. The Memorial Building, which features five sculptured panels that depict various scenes from Lincoln's youth, was completed in 1943. The Cabin Site Memorial features a bronze casting of the base logs and fireplace hearthstones that represent a cabin the Lincolns started in 1829 but never finished.

Best Time to Visit: The best time to visit is during the spring or fall when the temperatures are milder.

Pass/Permit/Fees: There is no fee to visit the Lincoln Boyhood National Memorial.

Closest City or Town: Lincoln City

Physical Address: 3027 E. S Street, Lincoln City, IN 47552

GPS Coordinates: 38.11452° N. 86.99670° W

Did You Know? The Lincoln Living Historical Farm is a working farm that has a log cabin, livestock, crops, and gardens. It is on the memorial grounds.

Clifty Falls State Park

This 570-acre park was gifted to the state of Indiana by the citizens of Madison, Indiana in 1920 to be the site of the first of four state parks with a naturalist program. Park features include Clifty Creek, Little Clifty Creek, and Clifty Creek Canyon, which crosses the entire north–south length of the park. There are also four waterfalls: Big Clifty Falls and Little Clifty Falls at 60 feet, Hoffman Falls at 78 feet, and Tunnel Falls with a drop of 83 feet. For hikers, there are ten trails that vary in difficulty from easy to moderate, rugged to very rugged. The only trail that's rated very rugged is Trail 2, and it is the most difficult trail in the state. In fact, the end of the trail is no longer open to the public due to the danger of falling rocks.

Best Time to Visit: It's best to visit after heavy rain when the falls are at their best.

Pass/Permit/Fees: There is a $7 fee for in-state vehicles and a $9 fee for out-of-state vehicles. There is also a $2 fee per person for walk-ins.

Closest City or Town: Madison

Physical Address: 1501 Green Road, Madison, IN 47250

GPS Coordinates: 38.75478° N, 85.42092° W

Did You Know? The Clifty Creek Canyon is situated so that the sun only shines in the canyon at midday. The upper rim is 800 feet above sea level, and it descends into the Ohio River Valley, which is 500 feet above sea level. The creek eventually drains into the Ohio River.

Marengo Cave

Marengo Cave is one of the four caves on the Indiana Cave Trail, but it can be visited on its own. Guests can take two walking tours to view the cave's massive rooms and spectacular formations. The Crystal Palace is a 40-minute tour that's rated easy and is perfect for families with small children. View the gigantic flowstone deposits on this tour. The Dripstone Trail is a little more difficult, but it still has an easy rating. This 60-minute tour is a great way to see totem pole stalagmites, soda straws, and the famous Penny Ceiling. More challenging adventures await those who choose the Waterfall Crawl, Beyond the Falls, or Underground Adventure tours that take guests to the muddy, wet, and undeveloped parts of the cave.

Best Time to Visit: Marengo Cave is open for tours Monday through Friday from 9:00 a.m. to 6:00 p.m. and Saturday and Sunday from 9:00 a.m. to 6:30 p.m.

Pass/Permit/Fees: The Crystal Palace Tour is $18.95 for adults and $10.95 for children ages 4 to 12. The Dripstone Trail is $21.95 for adults and $12.95 for children ages 4 to 12. Children ages 3 and under are free for both.

Closest City or Town: Marengo

Physical Address: 400 East State Rd 64, Marengo, IN 47140

GPS Coordinates: 38.37405° N, 86.33839° W

Did You Know? The Marengo Cave is advertised as "Indiana's Most Visited Natural Attraction."

Garfield Trail

Jim Davis—creator of Garfield the Cat, one of the world's most popular comic strip characters—calls Grant County, Indiana home. In honor of Garfield's enduring popularity, visitors can spend the day visiting 14 statues that depict the feline in various outfits and locations. Find these larger-than-life statues throughout Grant County, starting with the *Paws for Thought* statue in Marion and then following the trail to see these other statues: *Cool Cat, Gone Fishin'*, *Scream for Ice Cream, Worldly Cat, Glassblower, British Soldier, Firefighter, Medical Professional, Fit for Life*, *Bookworm, Duffer, College Bound*, and *Speedking*.

Along the way, explore a 1916 wooden caboose, the Buren Public Library, the Fairmount Historical Museum, Jonesboro City Hall, the Gas City-Mill Township Public Library, and Ivanhoe's Restaurant.

Best Time to Visit: The best time to visit the Garfield Trail is during the spring or fall when the weather is mild.

Pass/Permit/Fees: There is no fee to visit the Garfield Trail.

Closest City or Town: Marion

Physical Address: 505 W. 3rd Street, Marion, IN 46952

GPS Coordinates: 40.55926° N, 85.66472° W

Did You Know? Fairmont, Indiana is the hometown of Jim Davis, and it's also where his PAWS, Inc. studio is located.

Turkey Run State Park

Consistently rated as the number one state park in Indiana, Turkey Run has been in existence since 1916 and has more than 1 million visitors every year. Hiking, horseback riding, camping, swimming, visiting historic sites, fishing, canoeing, and kayaking are popular activities at Turkey Run. More than 14 miles of hiking trails wind through the park, ranging from easy to very rugged.

The Lieber Cabin, the Log Church, the Lusk Home, and the Narrows Covered Bridge are historic sites in the park that were built in the 1800s and early 1900s. They can be explored to learn more about the state's pioneer heritage. In Sugar Creek, one of the most scenic rivers in Indiana, anglers can catch bluegill, bass, and other fish.

Best Time to Visit: The best time to visit Turkey Run State Park is during the spring, summer, or fall.

Pass/Permit/Fees:
There is a $7 fee for in-state vehicles and a $9 fee for out-of-state vehicles. There is also a $2 fee per person for walk-ins.

Closest City or Town: Marshall

Physical Address: 8121 Park Road, Marshall, IN 47859

GPS Coordinates: 39.89095° N, 87.20095° W

Did You Know? Tennis courts, basketball courts, and sand volleyball courts are also available to visitors who bring their own equipment.

Spring Mill State Park

Spring Mill State Park was once a village that was founded in the 1800s due to its proximity to the water flowing from cave springs in the area. The constant, never-freezing water source provided power to numerous gristmills, a saw mill, a wool mill, and a distillery. Visitors can visit Pioneer Village, which has been fully restored to tell the story of the inhabitants of 1814 Spring Mill.

There are 20 historic structures to explore, including a 3-story limestone gristmill that dates back to 1817. The amazing aspect of this mill is that it is still grinding cornmeal today. Twin Caves is open for boat tours between Memorial Day and mid-October for guests ages 3 and above.

Best Time to Visit: The best time to visit Spring Mill State Park is during the summer when you can tour the cave.

Pass/Permit/Fees: There is a $7 fee per in-state vehicle and a $9 fee per out-of-state vehicle to visit Spring Mill State Park. Cave tours by boat are $13 per person.

Closest City or Town: Mitchell

Physical Address: 3333 IN-60 East, Mitchell, IN 47446

GPS Coordinates: 38.73183° N, 86.41835° W

Did You Know? The Grissom Memorial in Spring Mill State Park is open daily year round to honor Indiana native astronaut Virgil "Gus" Grissom, the second man in space.

Brown County State Park

This 15,696-acre state park offers a little something for everyone. There are 70 miles of horseback-riding trails, 30 miles of biking trails, and 18 miles of hiking trails. You can ride your own horse or enjoy a guided ride from the on-premises Saddle Barn. The park contains two lakes that are perfect for fishing (even in the winter), a nature center with various exhibits, an Olympic-size swimming pool, campsites, picnic areas, tennis courts, and more.

This park first opened to the public in 1929, and as the site became more popular, additional amenities were added. Be sure to check out Weed Patch Hill, which, at 1,058 feet in elevation, is one of the highest points in the state.

Best Time to Visit: The best time to visit Brown County State Park is during the spring, summer, or fall.

Pass/Permit/Fees: There is a $7 fee for in-state vehicles and a $9 fee for out-of-state vehicles. There is also a $2 fee per person for walk-ins.

Closest City or Town: Nashville

Physical Address: 1801 Indiana 46 East, Nashville, IN 47448

GPS Coordinates: 39.17954° N, 86.27033° W

Did You Know? Brown County State Park is nicknamed the "Little Smokies" because the area resembles the Great Smoky Mountains in North Carolina and Tennessee.

Yellowwood State Forest

Established in 1940, Yellowwood State Forest was initially leased to the state of Indiana by the federal government. It was officially deeded to the state in 1956 after the Civilian Conservation Corps and Works Project Administration had created three lakes, a residence, and a shelter house on the 2,000 acres of land. In addition, the abandoned and eroded soil had been replenished by planting thousands of trees, including red pine, jack pine, white pine, jack pine, shortleaf pine, scotch pine, black walnut, black locust, white oak, and red oak. Only red and white pines were found suitable for the northern climate; the others are succumbing to disease, insects, and the harsh winters. Yellowwood, the largest of the three lakes, was completed in 1939 at 133 acres across and 30 feet deep. The forest is a popular place for recreation, particularly hiking, horseback riding, boating, and camping.

Best Time to Visit: Visit Yellowwood State Forest during the spring or fall when the temperatures are milder.

Pass/Permit/Fees: There is no fee to visit the forest.

Closest City or Town: Nashville

Physical Address: 772 Yellowwood Lake Road, Nashville, IN 47448

GPS Coordinates: 39.18398° N, 86.33839° W

Did You Know? The Yellowwood State Forest covers more than 25,000 acres.

Newburgh Museum

This history museum is designed to preserve, exhibit, and educate visitors about the history and culture of Newburgh, Indiana and the surrounding area. As a river town, Newburgh has been in existence since at least 1803. It's possible that the Shawnee Native Americans and the prehistoric Mississippian culture flourished in the area even earlier, perhaps even before 1450 CE.

The museum chronicles the town's founding, the origins of its name, its role in industry, its period of decline, and its rebirth to become what it is now. Permanent exhibits include the *E&OV Depot*, *Town's Founding*, and *Early Industry*, among others. The real attraction in this museum is its rotating exhibits, which have included *Newburgh Rocks*, a tribute to Marcia Yockey, *Coal Mining*, and *Cypress Beach*, among others.

Best Time to Visit: The Newburgh Museum is open Friday and Saturday from 11:00 a.m. to 3:00 p.m.

Pass/Permit/Fees: There is no fee to visit the Newburgh Museum, but donations are appreciated.

Closest City or Town: Newburgh

Physical Address: 503 State Street, Newburgh, IN 47630

GPS Coordinates: 37.94921° N, 87.40472° W

Did You Know? On the first Sunday of each month, the Newburgh Museum hosts a guest speaker to share stories of Newburgh's history.

Ohio River Scenic Byway

Designated as one of the first 14 National Scenic Byways in the country in 1996, the Ohio River Scenic Byway is lined with farm markets, artist studios, antique shops, historic mansions, artisan wineries, and quaint bed-and-breakfast inns. The byway is 302 miles long in Indiana, allowing travelers to explore southern Indiana in the most picturesque way possible. More than 60 interpretive panels provide interesting facts about the area. You can find these panels at various points of interest, such as the Utopian society of New Harmony, ancient fossils at the Falls of the Ohio State Park, the Underground Railroad in Madison, and Abraham Lincoln history in Spencer County. There is also plenty of adventure to be found on the Ohio River Scenic Byway, from cave exploration to ziplining and beyond.

Best Time to Visit: Drive the Ohio River Scenic Byway in the fall, when the leaves are changing colors.

Pass/Permit/Fees: There is no fee to drive the byway.

Closest City or Town: Newburgh

Physical Address: Ohio River Scenic Byway, Newburgh, IN 47630

GPS Coordinates: 37.94540° N, 87.40522° W

Did You Know? If you want to travel the entire length of the Ohio River Scenic Byway, allow at least 2 days to enjoy all the sites because it is 943 miles long and passes through three states.

Snite Museum of Art

The Snite Museum of Art, on the campus of the University of Notre Dame, has more than 25,000 works of art from multiple cultures, media, and eras. It is meant to provide a resource for art appreciation, lectures, workshops, programs, and exhibitions. The museum opened in 1980, becoming the first art museum at Notre Dame. Before that, the school used various public spaces to display art. The Fred B. Snite family donated funds in 1975 to build the museum, which includes the Mestrovic sculpture studio and the O'Shaughnessy art gallery. Designed by Ambrose Richardson, the 70,000-square-foot building is a work of art in itself.

Best Time to Visit: The Snite Museum of Art is open Tuesday, Wednesday, and Friday from 10:00 a.m. to 5:00 p.m. On Thursday, it is open late until 7:30 p.m. On Saturday, it's open from 12:00 p.m. to 5:00 p.m. except when there are home football games.

Pass/Permit/Fees: There is no fee to visit the museum.

Closest City or Town: Notre Dame

Physical Address: 100 Moose Krause Circle, Notre Dame, IN 46556

GPS Coordinates: 41.70036° N, 86.23578° W

Did You Know? The Charles B. Hayes Family Sculpture Park, an 8-acre site designed by architect Michael Van Valkenburgh, is on the grounds of the Snite Museum of Art.

Wilstem Wildlife Park

Wilstem Wildlife Park offers various adventures within its 1,100 acres of secluded woodlands, meadows, and gentle hills. Among them are a Drive-Thru Safari, a 4,000-foot-long canopy-tour zip line, hiking trails, a swimming pool, horseback-riding trails, and guided ATV tours. The Drive-Thru Safari is the feature activity. You can stay in your personal vehicle or take a guided tour on the Safari Wagon to view more than 40 species of animals.

Alpacas, zebras, sloths, giraffes, kangaroos, and grizzly bears are just some of the animals you'll spot while enjoying the Indiana woodlands. You can purchase tickets to Exclusive Encounters to gain VIP access to many park creatures. The Safari Wagon tour includes feed and carrots to give to the animals that wander up to your window.

Best Time to Visit: The Drive-Thru Safari is open daily from 9:30 a.m. to 4:00 p.m.

Pass/Permit/Fees: Personal vehicle tours are $17 for adults, $15 for seniors ages 65 and older, and $12 for children between the ages of 3 and 12. Guided Wagon tours are $29 for adults, $27 for seniors, and $24 for children.

Closest City or Town: Paoli

Physical Address: 4229 US-150 West, Paoli, IN 47454

GPS Coordinates: 38.56859° N, 86.54064° W

Did You Know? Grizzly Ridge and Roos & Crew are two live animal attractions included with admission.

Seven Pillars

Known locally as "The Cliffs," the Seven Pillars is a formation that developed over centuries from the wind and water eroding the limestone on the north bluff of the Mississinewa River. The perfectly sculpted pillars, which appear to be holding up the bluff, are best viewed from the south bank of the Mississinewa River. If you want to check out the view from atop the Seven Pillars, take the Frances Slocum Trail, which follows the north bank of the river and passes along the top of the pillars. The Miami Native American tribe has long considered this formation sacred and often held council meetings in the alcoves, especially during early contact with European settlers. They even operated a trading post from near the pillars at one time. The Miami tribe still owns land on the river's south bank, where the sacred longhouse is located.

Best Time to Visit: Visit in late summer when the Miami Heritage Days at the Pillars festival is held. If you want to avoid crowds, visit during the spring or fall.

Pass/Permit/Fees: There is no fee to visit the Seven Pillars.

Closest City or Town: Peru

Physical Address: 3667 Mississinewa Road, Peru, IN 46970

GPS Coordinates: 40.72678° N, 85.99505° W

Did You Know? The Seven Pillars was named the top Wonder of Miami County in 2005.

Cowles Bog

This 4,000-year-old wetland in Indiana Dunes National Park allowed ecologist Henry Chandler Cowles to conduct innovative work in ecological succession, which eventually drew international attention to the area and led to preservation efforts for the Indiana Dunes. In 1965, Cowles Bog was named a National Natural Landmark. The bog contains important ecological habitats, including fen, marsh, wet meadow, swamp, pond, and, of course, bog habitats. The main body of the Cowles Bog is made up of muck from woody and marsh plants that have grown into the area. The bog is covered with a thick layer of leaf litter that covers a thin topsoil layer. This bog supports mostly bird and insect life, but visitors will occasionally spot whitetail deer in the area as well.

Best Time to Visit: The best time to visit Cowles Bog is during the spring, summer, or fall.

Pass/Permit/Fees: There is no fee to visit Cowles Bog.

Closest City or Town: Porter

Physical Address: 1050 N. Mineral Springs Road, Dune Acres, IN 46304

GPS Coordinates: 41.64365° N, 87.09375° W

Did You Know? Cowles Bog Trail is a 4.7-mile lollipop trail that follows gravel at the edge of the bog. You'll pass through black oak savanna and between interdunal ponds. At the apex of the final dune, you'll be rewarded with an incredible view of Lake Michigan.

Indiana Dunes State Park

Located near Lake Michigan in northern Indiana, the 2,182-acre Indiana Dunes State Park is a recreational paradise for beach-goers, hikers, and nature enthusiasts. The sand dunes, which have taken thousands of years to form, rise 200 feet above Lake Michigan and provide a wide variety of habitats for diverse wildlife. Numerous plants grow in the park, many of which serve as stabilization for the sand. The park passes along over 3 miles of beach along the southern shore of Lake Michigan. It's a popular spot for swimming in the summer. Indiana Dunes State Park was established in 1925 for recreational purposes, allowing people to splash in the lake or explore the sand dunes on foot or bike. In the winter, the park is open for cross-country skiing and snowshoeing, but snowmobiles are prohibited.

Best Time to Visit: The best time to visit Indiana Dunes State Park is in the summer for swimming and hiking or in the winter for cross-country skiing and snowshoeing.

Pass/Permit/Fees: There is a $7 fee for in-state vehicles and a $12 fee for out-of-state vehicles.

Closest City or Town: Porter

Physical Address: 1600 N. 25 East, Chesterton, IN 46304

GPS Coordinates: 41.66249° N, 87.03974° W

Did You Know? This area is home to both a state and national park. The passes for the national park do not gain you entrance to the state park.

Thistlethwaite Falls

As one of the top waterfalls in Indiana, Thistlethwaite Falls is much more than just a beautiful waterfall; it's also a great place to search for ancient fossils. The waterfall was formed in 1854 when Timothy Thistlethwaite used damming techniques to create a new channel in the West Fork of the Whitewater River. He needed more water to power his sawmill, which was located nearby. He then constructed several more mills in the area that were also powered by the falls. The mills no longer exist, but the waterfall remains. It's a simple hike to reach the falls, with just a basic trail and stairway leading above and down to the base. There is also a bridge that will give you access to a walking path to the base on the opposite side of the river. The bridge is narrow and has no shoulder, so it is considered the more dangerous route of the two.

Best Time to Visit: Visit in the spring when the water is running higher and faster.

Pass/Permit/Fees: There is no fee to visit the falls.

Closest City or Town: Richmond

Physical Address: 65 Waterfall Road, Richmond, IN 47374

GPS Coordinates: 38.84804° N, 84.89817

Did You Know? In addition to his sawmill, Timothy Thistlethwaite built a grist mill, paper mill, and flour mill in the Happy Hollow district of what would become Richmond. They were all powered by the 47-foot falls.

Holiday World & Splashin' Safari

This combination water park and theme park is divided into four areas that celebrate U.S. holidays: Christmas, Thanksgiving, Halloween, and the Fourth of July. Enjoy rides, games, water slides, entertainment, and culinary delights while visiting this park. Be sure to ride the three wooden coasters (the Legend, the Raven, and the Voyage), and the two steel coasters (Thunderbird and The Howler).

The water park features a safari theme and boasts the two longest water coasters in the world (the Wildebeest and the Mammoth). The theme park and water park also offer several raft rides, wave pools, a junior wave pool, two child-sized water slide areas, a lazy river, and a family "tipping bucket" attraction.

Best Time to Visit: The best time to visit Holiday World & Splashin' Safari is in the summer.

Pass/Permit/Fees: The charge to visit Holiday World & Splashin' Safari varies. See the website for ticket prices on the date you want to visit.

Closest City or Town: Santa Claus

Physical Address: 452 E. Christmas Boulevard, Santa Claus, IN 47579

GPS Coordinates: 38.11939° N, 86.91560° W

Did You Know? Holiday World & Splashin' Safari was formerly known as Santa Claus Land, a project first conceived in 1941 by Louis J. Koch.

Santa Claus Museum & Village

The town of Santa Claus is a popular place for fans of Santa Claus, the mythical character who brings children Christmas presents. The Santa Claus Museum & Village traces the history of the city from its humble beginnings as the tiny settlement of Santa Fee (its former name) to the present day. You'll examine historical documents, artifacts, and photographs that tell the story of how the town got its name, its tourism history, and the town's unique heritage. The museum has thousands of letters to Santa Claus on file, along with audio recordings of Jim Yellig, who was the town's official Santa Claus for 54 years. Antique toys and a massive Santa collection are also on display, and there's even the original Santa Claus Post Office, where you can write your own free letter to Santa Claus. If you include your full address, Santa and his elves will send a letter back to you in December.

Best Time to Visit: The Santa Claus Museum & Village is open Saturday and Sunday from 9:00 a.m. to 4:00 p.m.

Pass/Permit/Fees: There is no fee to visit the Santa Claus Museum & Village.

Closest City or Town: Santa Claus

Physical Address: 69 IN-245, Santa Claus, IN 47579

GPS Coordinates: 38.11604° N, 86.90955° W

Did You Know? In addition to the Post Office, the Village is home to a historic 1935 Santa Claus statue and the 1880 Santa Claus Church.

Jug Rock

Situated just outside of Shoals, Indiana, Jug Rock is a sandstone formation that ranks as the largest freestanding table-rock formation east of the Mississippi River. Part of the Mansfield Formation, Jug Rock developed between 325 and 286 million years ago. It became separated from a nearby cliff when erosion caused fracture lines in the area. The rock formation is oddly placed in the woodlands of south-central Indiana, which is why it garners attention from both geologists and visitors.

Although it somewhat resembles a jug, it looks more closely like a giant table, which is why it is generally referred to as a table-rock formation. It is unique east of the Mississippi because most rock is protected from erosion forces by dense forests and rolling hills. Typically, formations such as this do not last long in this area because of extreme climate fluctuations, which makes Jug Rock even more of an anomaly.

Best Time to Visit: The best time to visit Jug Rock is in the spring or fall when the weather is cooler.

Pass/Permit/Fees: There is no fee to visit Jug Rock.

Closest City or Town: Shoals

Physical Address: 722 Albright Lane, Shoals, IN 47581

GPS Coordinates: 38.67667° N, 86.79729° W

Did You Know? Jug Rock is such a source of local pride that it is the mascot of Shoals High School.

Cataract Falls

By volume, the two sets of waterfalls that make up Cataract Falls are the largest waterfalls in Indiana. They are the result of pre-glacial bedrock ridges buried underneath ancient lake sediment. The first waterfall, known as the Upper Falls, drops 45 feet, and the Lower Falls drops 30 feet. A walking trail connects the two waterfalls, but you can also drive to both. The trail is rated easy, so walking between the waterfalls should not be too tricky. You have to visit the Lieber State Recreation Area to see the waterfalls, but the gorge just below the Upper Falls can be viewed without visiting the park. The waterfalls empty into the southern end of Cagles Mill Lake.

Best Time to Visit: This waterfall flows all year, but it will be at its fullest after a heavy rain in the spring or summer.

Pass/Permit/Fees: There is a $7 fee for in-state vehicles and a $9 fee for out-of-state vehicles. There is also a $2 fee per person for walk-ins.

Closest City or Town: Spencer

Physical Address: 2605 N. Cataract Road, Spencer, IN 47460

GPS Coordinates: 39.43510° N, 86.81486° W

Did You Know? A wooden bridge that once crossed Mill Creek between the two falls was washed out during a flood in 1875. The Cataract Bridge was constructed at the Upper Falls in 1876 and was used until 1988. The Cataract Bridge was restored in 1995 and is still in use today.

McCormick's Creek State Park

Named for John McCormick, the first settler in the Bloomington area, McCormick's Creek State Park is the oldest in the state. It was dedicated on July 4, 1916 to mark the state's centennial year. McCormick originally settled in 1816 on 100 acres along the canyon near the waterfalls, which are still a main attraction at the park. Before McCormick arrived in the area, the land served as hunting grounds for the Miami Native American tribe. The upper portions of the canyon are approximately 700 feet above sea level, and there are more than 10 miles of hiking trails throughout the park, including Wolf Cave Nature Preserve Trail #5 (rated moderate) and McCormick's Creek Falls Trail #3 (rated rugged). Anglers enjoy fishing for largemouth bass, crappie, catfish, carp, and freshwater drum from the White River.

Best Time to Visit: Visit during the spring or summer following heavy rain when the waterfalls run strong.

Pass/Permit/Fees: There is no fee to visit McCormick's Creek State Park.

Closest City or Town: Spencer

Physical Address: 250 McCormick Creek Park Road, Spencer, IN 47460

GPS Coordinates: 39.29830° N, 86.72451° W

Did You Know? McCormick's Creek State Park is just over 350 acres in area and continues to grow as surrounding farms are put up for sale.

Studebaker National Museum

Automobile enthusiasts will love the Studebaker National Museum, which is committed to sharing the story of Studebaker vehicles and the industrial heritage of South Bend, Indiana. Established in 2005, the museum boasts 55,000 square feet of fully climate-controlled exhibition space and storage facilities to ensure the preservation of the museum's priceless collection. Of special interest are seven artifacts that have been designated as National Treasures, including the carriage that carried President Abraham Lincoln to Ford's Theater on the night he was assassinated and a carriage that Marquis de Lafayette used on his 1824 farewell tour of the U.S. The Lafayette carriage has been in the possession of the Clement Studebaker family since he purchased it in 1887 and the Lincoln carriage since 1890.

Best Time to Visit: The Studebaker National Museum is open Monday through Saturday from 10:00 a.m. to 5:00 p.m. and Sunday from 12:00 p.m. to 5:00 p.m.

Pass/Permit/Fees: Admission is $10 for adults, $6 for students ages 6 to 17, $8.50 for seniors ages 60 and up, and free for children ages 5 and under.

Closest City or Town: South Bend

Physical Address: 201 Chapin Street, South Bend, IN 46601

GPS Coordinates: 41.67553° N, 86.26157° W

Did You Know? The Studebaker vehicle collection was donated to South Bend in 1966.

University of Notre Dame

Founded in 1842 by Rev. Edward F. Sorin, a priest at the Congregation of Holy Cross French missionary order, the University of Notre Dame is a Catholic university that serves about 8,500 students each year. The university was governed by the priest at Holy Cross until 1967, when governance was transferred to a board of trustees made up of both lay and religious representatives. While the university has many strong areas, it is particularly known for its departments of philosophy and theology, and as a leading undergraduate teaching school.

In addition, it has long been at the forefront of research, having pioneered the transmission of wireless messages, the formula for synthetic rubber, and the aerodynamics of glider flights, to name a few. Most students live on the Notre Dame campus because participating in campus living is considered a major part of the Notre Dame experience.

Best Time to Visit: The best time to tour the University of Notre Dame campus is during the fall or spring semesters.

Pass/Permit/Fees: There is no fee to visit the university.

Closest City or Town: South Bend

Physical Address: Notre Dame, IN 46556

GPS Coordinates: 41.69979° N, 86.23876° W

Did You Know? *U.S. News & World Report*, Niche, and *Forbes* magazine have all ranked the University of Notre Dame among the top 25 universities in the country.

George Rogers Clark National Historical Park

This park is named for the American colonel who captured Fort Sackville in 1779. Because of Clark's military campaign, the British were forced to cede a vast territory to the United States.

The park offers lessons about 18th-century frontier life as well as opportunities for family and recreational time. A picnic area is located near the visitor center parking area, and sidewalks lead to a variety of monuments and statues. The grounds include formally designed plantings installed during various periods of site development.

Best Time to Visit: The best time to visit is during the spring or fall when the weather is milder.

Pass/Permit/Fees: There is no fee to visit the George Rogers Clark National Historical Park.

Closest City or Town: Vincennes

Physical Address: 401 S. 2nd Street, Vincennes, IN 47591

GPS Coordinates: 38.67810° N, 87.53675° W

Did You Know? The territory ceded included Indiana, Illinois, Michigan, Ohio, Wisconsin, and parts of Minnesota.

Pine Hills Nature Preserve

Pine Hills Nature Preserve was the first dedicated nature preserve in the state, earning that designation in 1969, a year after being named a National Natural Landmark. Its scenery is spectacular, with craggy hills, hogback ridges, deep gorges, and towering sandstone bluffs covered with evergreens and hardwood trees. The 470-acre preserve has been untouched except for trail maintenance and the addition of a few signs and some stairs. Before European settlers entered the area in the 1820s, Native Americans and French explorers traversed the land. Visitors today pass through a dense hemlock grove and alongside a swift-moving creek. The park has several natural features as well, including The Slide, Honeycomb Rock, Devil's Backbone, and numerous others.

Best Time to Visit: The best time to visit Pine Hills Nature Preserve is during the spring or fall when the weather is milder.

Pass/Permit/Fees: There is a $7 fee for in-state vehicles and a $9 fee for out-of-state vehicles to visit Shades State Park, where the preserve is located. There is also a $2 fee per person for walk-ins.

Closest City or Town: Waveland

Physical Address: IN-234, Waveland, IN 47989

GPS Coordinates: 39.94268° N, 87.04886° W

Did You Know? There are carvings from earlier visitors on Devil's Backbone, some dating back to the 1800s.

Williamsport Falls

Near the center of Williamsport is Williamsport Falls, a 90-foot waterfall that is the highest in Indiana. Fall Creek flows through the town, crosses a railroad, and falls over a sandstone ledge. In the 19th century, the water flow over the ledge could power a mill located below the waterfall, but in the intervening years, the flow has become inconsistent and often slows to a trickle. The reason for this is that industrial farms in the area have diverted the natural water flow from the creek for irrigation and other purposes. In fact, the waterfall is often referred to by locals as "Dry Falls." A trail leads down Fall Creek to the gorge where the falls are located. You can also explore behind the falls if you're willing to get a little wet. Even if the water isn't flowing during your visit, the caprock over the falls is impressive and picturesque.

Best Time to Visit: The best time to visit Williamsport Falls is after heavy rain or snow.

Pass/Permit/Fees: There is no fee to visit Williamsport Falls.

Closest City or Town: Williamsport

Physical Address: 25 N. Monroe Street, Williamsport, IN 47993

GPS Coordinates: 40.28709° N, 87.29297° W

Did You Know? The actual height of Williamsport Falls has changed over the years as chunks of the ledge have detached from the rock and fallen to the bottom.

Proper Planning

With this guide, you are well on your way to properly planning a marvelous adventure. When you plan your travels, you should become familiar with the area, save any maps to your phone for access without internet, and bring plenty of water—especially during the summer months. Depending on which adventure you choose, you will also want to bring snacks or even a lunch. For younger children, you should do your research and find destinations that best suit your family's needs. You should also plan when and where to get gas, local lodgings, and food. We've done our best to group these destinations based on nearby towns and cities to help make planning easier.

Dangerous Wildlife

There are several dangerous animals and insects you may encounter while hiking. With a good dose of caution and awareness, you can explore safely. Here are steps you can take to keep yourself and your loved ones safe from dangerous flora and fauna while exploring:

- Keep to the established trails.
- Do not look under rocks, leaves, or sticks.
- Keep hands and feet out of small crawl spaces, bushes, covered areas, or crevices.
- Wear long sleeves and pants to keep arms and legs protected.
- Keep your distance should you encounter any dangerous wildlife or plants.

Limited Cell Service

Do not rely on cell service for navigation or emergencies. Always have a map with you, and let someone know where you are and how long you intend to be gone, just in case.

First Aid Information

Always travel with a first aid kit in case of emergencies.

Here are items you should be certain to include in your primary first aid kit:

- Nitrile gloves
- Blister care products
- Band-Aids in multiple sizes, waterproof type
- Ace wrap and athletic tape
- Alcohol wipes and antibiotic ointment
- Irrigation syringe
- Tweezers, nail clippers, trauma shears, safety pins
- Small zip-lock bags to hold contaminated trash

It's also a good practice to keep a secondary first aid kit, especially when hiking, for more serious injuries or medical emergencies. Items in this should include:

- Blood clotting sponges
- Sterile gauze pads
- Trauma pads
- Moist burn pads

- Triangular bandages/sling
- Butterfly strips
- Tincture of benzoin
- Medications (ibuprofen, acetaminophen, antihistamine, aspirin, etc.)
- Thermometer
- CPR mask
- Wilderness medicine handbook
- Antivenin

There is much more to explore, but this is a great start.

For information on all national parks, visit https://www.nps.gov/index.htm.

This site will give you information on up-to-date entrance fees and how to purchase a park pass for unlimited access to national and state parks. This site will also introduce you to all of the trails at each park.

Always check before you travel to destinations to make sure there are no closures. Some hiking trails close when there is heavy rain or snow in the area and other parks close parts of their land to allow wildlife to migrate. Attractions may change their hours or temporarily shut down for various reasons. Check the websites for the most up-to-date information.

Made in the USA
Monee, IL
19 June 2023

36215160R00077